More praise for *Seeing God*

"I have had the privilege of studying on a weekly basis with Rabbi Aaron. His inspiration and wisdom shed new light on the oldest secrets of all." —The Honorable Ehud Olmert, mayor of Jerusalem

"Cogent, lucid, and very readable . . . I love, love, love this book." —Yitta Halberstam, bestselling author of *Small Miracles*

"Superb . . . In *Seeing God*, Rabbi David Aaron urges us to see, within the demands of daily life, the divine context of all existence, and he provides markers for the path we must follow to achieve this goal." —Dr. Gerald Schroeder, author of *The Hidden Face of God*

"[Aaron] succeeds in presenting one of Kabbalah's most perplexing notions in plain language that can be readily grasped." —*Publishers Weekly*

"*Seeing God* is a down-to-earth look at Judaism's Kabbalah. . . . Aaron offers anecdotes from his life that make the material interesting and approachable." —*Spokesman-Review*

"A much-needed book today, *Seeing God* will open your eyes to experiencing your life in new ways." —Rabbi Simon Jacobson, author of *Toward a Meaningful Life*

continued on next page . . .

Praise for *Endless Light*

"[Rabbi David Aaron] offers answers from the Torah . . . in an easy-to-read popular style, with reminders that Kabbalah is about receiving, about making a place in yourself in which you can receive what life has to offer."

—*The Jewish Advocate*

"It's not just celebrities Diane Ladd, Roseanne, Madonna, Kirk Douglas and Jeff Goldblum. All types of people, Jews and non-Jews alike, are being drawn to Kabbalah, the Jewish mystical tradition that blends astrology, astral travel, numerology, physics, psychology, reincarnation and magic. Aaron offers a simplified application of the esoteric teachings to modern situations." —*The Washington Post*

"Rabbi Aaron blends anecdotes, biblical stories and Kabbalah's wisdom to guide readers on their spiritual journey. The book not only helps answer some of life's more nagging questions, but also inspires personal growth while mapping out guidelines for healthy familial relationships."

—*Baltimore Jewish Times*

"David Aaron . . . taps the great mystical power of the Kabbalah to offer insights into living everyday life with love and power. . . . Aaron's meditations are grounded solidly in the Jewish Kabbalistic tradition." —*Publishers Weekly*

"Media with a message . . . [*Endless Light*] focuses on spiritual growth, personal power and choices."

—*The Atlanta Journal-Constitution*

"By his writing, speaking and other efforts, including his institute in the Old City of Jerusalem known as Isralight, Aaron is trying to spread Kabbalah in a meaningful, reverent yet accessible way." —*St. Louis Post-Dispatch*

ALSO BY DAVID AARON

Endless Light

Seeing God

TEN LIFE-CHANGING LESSONS
OF THE KABBALAH

Rabbi David Aaron

BERKLEY BOOKS, NEW YORK

Most Berkley Books are available at special quantity discounts for bulk purchases for sales promotions, premiums, fund-raising, or educational use. Special books, or book excerpts, can also be created to fit specific needs.

For details, write: Special Markets, The Berkley Publishing Group, 375 Hudson Street, New York, New York 10014.

A Berkley Book
Published by The Berkley Publishing Group
A division of Penguin Putnam Inc.
375 Hudson Street
New York, New York 10014

Book design by Debbie Glasserman
Cover design by Teresa Bonner

PRINTING HISTORY
Jeremy P. Tarcher/Putnam hardcover edition / January 2001
Berkley trade paperback edition / January 2002

Berkley trade paperback ISBN: 0-425-18320-3

Visit our website at
www.penguinputnam.com

The Library of Congress has catalogued the
Jeremy P. Tarcher/Putnam hardcover edition as follows:

Aaron, David.
Seeing God : ten life-changing lessons of
the Kabbalah/David Aaron.
p. cm.
ISBN 1-58542-080-8
1. God (Judaism) 2. Spiritual life—Judaism. 3. Cabala. I. Title.
BM610.A25 2001 00-061515
296.3'11—dc21

PRINTED IN THE UNITED STATES OF AMERICA

10 9 8 7 6 5 4 3 2 1

Acknowledgments

Great thanks to my wife, Chana. Our life together has been an awesome, spiritual sight-seeing adventure, and she has shown me many of the sights.

Many, many thanks to my very talented editor, Sarah Rigler, who did an exceptional job in helping me put these secrets into writing. I am also very thankful to Uriela Obst for adding her professional touch, giving these ideas even greater clarity.

My deep appreciation to Denise Silvestro of Penguin Putnam for her expertise, advice, and critical eye.

I am extremely grateful to the many supporters of the Isralight Institute, whose generosity has provided me with the opportunity to present the ideas of this book. Special thanks to Dr. Herb Caskey,

Dr. Bob and Sarah Friedman, Moshe and Sarah Hermelin, and Aba and Pamela Claman for their consistent love and support.

I am also grateful to the many students who have attended my talks and seminars. Your receptivity has empowered me to access and share these sacred teachings.

I am forever in debt to my holy teachers, especially Rabbi Shlomo Fischer *Shlita,* for all their brilliance and sweetness.

Thank you, Hashem. You are the one and only Author. My entire being is filled with joy and gratitude to serve You.

Special thanks to my true friend Dr. Herb Caskey,
whose generosity made this project possible.
May the study of these secrets bring great merit to his parents,
Morris and Rose Caskey of blessed memory.

To my terrific parents,
Joe and Luba

To my phenomenal wife,
Chana

To my amazing children,
Lyadia, Ne'ema, Ananiel, Nuriel, Yehuda, Tzuriel, and Shmaya

contents

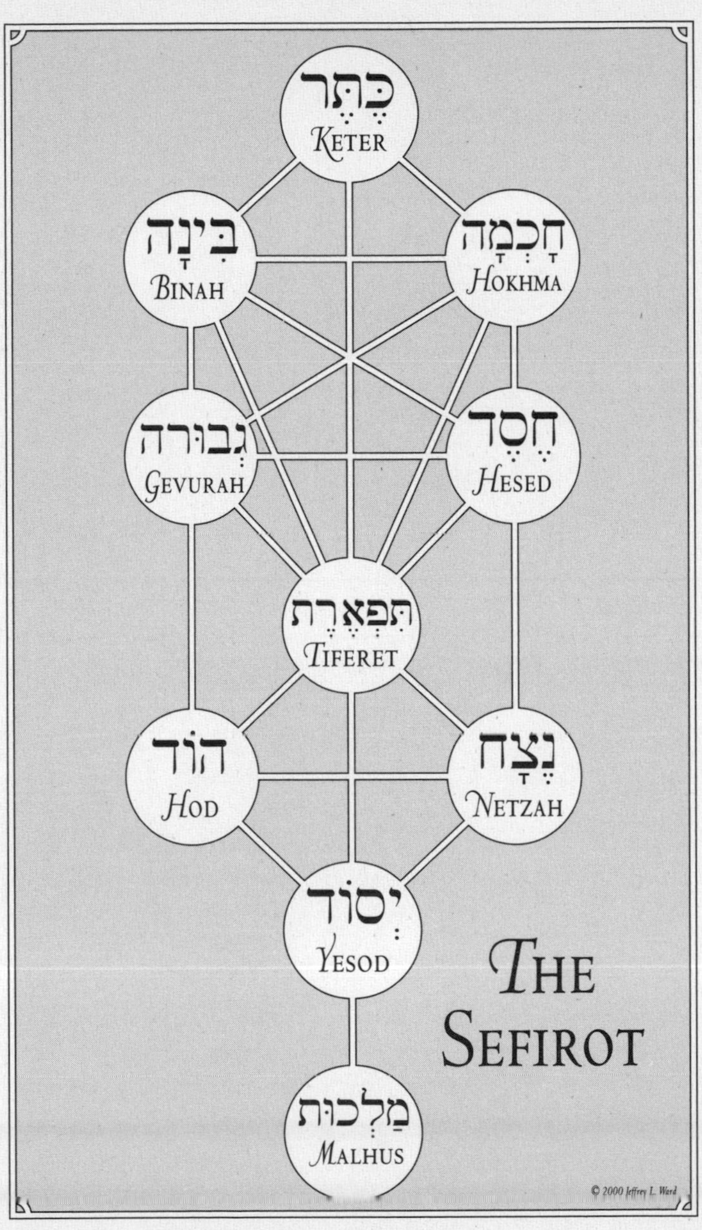
כֶּתֶר
KETER
בִּינָה
BINAH
חָכְמָה
HOKHMA
גְבוּרה
GEVURAH
חֶסֶד
HESED
תִּפְאֶרֶת
TIFERET
הוֹד
HOD
נֶצָח
NETZAH
יְסוֹד
YESOD
מַלְכוּת
MALHUS
THE SEFIROT
© 2000 Jeffrey L. Ward

Seeing God

GLASSES FOR YOUR SOUL

We have all been taught that we cannot see God, but the truth is not only that we can see God but that we have actually been looking at God the whole time. We just didn't see Who we were looking at.

If you wear corrective lenses, I am sure you can remember the time you got a new prescription and walked out onto the street. All of a sudden you saw a new world. It was actually the same old world but with new clarity and intensity. All this brilliant detail was before your very eyes all along, you just needed the right glasses to see.

God is right before your eyes—the eyes of your soul—and all you need are the right lenses through which to look.

This book will introduce you to a whole new vision. Life will never be the same. It will empower you to see in a whole new way. The wisdom contained here is drawn from the ancient teachings of the

Kabbalah—the mystical interpretation of the teachings of Moses, the prophet. I didn't invent these ideas. I only translated them into a language that anyone can understand and everyone can use.

But just a word of advice: Don't read this book. See through it. It's really not a book at all. It is glasses for your soul.

DAVID AARON

ISRALIGHT INSTITUTE

DAVID.AARON@ISRALIGHT.ORG

one

GETTING RID OF GOD

My three-year-old son was watching me pray one day, trying to imitate my movements, pretending he was also praying. Then out of the blue, he blurted out, "Daddy! I just saw God's feet."

I didn't know what my response should be to this, but quickly I decided that truth was my best option. "Yehuda," I said, "you couldn't have seen God's feet. God doesn't have feet."

He seemed startled by that, but all he said was, "Oh."

A couple of minutes went by, then he tugged at my sleeve. He looked at me with his big brown eyes and, smiling sweetly, said with total conviction, "But I saw them."

There was nothing I could do to persuade him otherwise. So I decided to let it ride. After all, he is only three years old. Hopefully, by the time he reaches adulthood he will have learned that God doesn't have feet. If he still harbors that concept, it will get in the way of his truly seeing God.

This is a problem I often encounter in the people who come to the Isralight Institute in Jerusalem, yearning to see God, but frustrated because in childhood they picked up concepts that in adulthood act as spiritual blindfolds.

People today truly want to meet God. They are looking less for an understanding of God than for an introduction to God. They want a personal audience. They want to see God. And surprising as it may sound, it is possible. God can be seen and wants to be seen.

But the sad fact is that most people don't see God, can't see God, even when they want to.

So before we begin to describe how God can be seen, we will address why we can't see Him. Hopefully, in so doing, we will unmask and remove the major obstacles that stand in our way.

Most of the people I have met during my years as a rabbi are wearing spiritual blindfolds. This causes them a lot of suffering, because these blindfolds block the eyes of the soul and they are never free to see God.

Some people are aware of the fact that they are walking blindly through life, but most are not. And if you don't know what's hurting you, it's harder to heal.

In my seminars I often ask people to write their definitions of God. Typical answers are intellectual, philosophical, abstract. Then I ask the participants to write a letter to God, starting with "Dear God, I always wanted to ask you . . ." I request that they write with the nondominant hand to simulate the experience of writing as a child, because the object of the exercise is to get at the earliest point in their lives, when they acquired their image of God.

And this is where the blindfolds reveal themselves. No matter what the person's intellectual understanding of God, their childlike emotional vision is revealed by letters like:

- "Dear God . . . why did you take my grandfather?"
- "Dear God . . . why do you allow wars to happen?"
- "Dear God . . . why are there so many bad people in the world?"

All negative associations, suggesting an unfair, merciless, punitive image of God.

Imagine if the way you dealt with money today were based on the way you understood money when you were five years old. What would you be spending your money on? Or, if your present diet were based on your understanding of nutrition when you were a child, how would you be eating today? So you can imagine that if your spiritual life is based on a childhood understanding of God, you might find your present search severely handicapped.

Purple Guy in the Sky

From time to time my wife and I sit with the kids and take a look at their latest drawings. Generally the pictures are pretty consistent—Daddy has the orange curly hair, the flowers are bigger than the people, and the shining sun has a big happy grin. But one day my five-year-old daughter Ne'ema brought us a drawing that in addition to the usual stuff featured a bizarre purple-green figure floating in the sky.

"Ne'ema," I asked, "who is this?"

She pretended not to hear my question and began talking about something else in the picture.

I was persistent until finally she couldn't escape identifying Mister X.

She motioned to me to come close, so she could whisper in my ear and protect her secret from her brothers and sisters close by. "It's God."

Of course my other kids would not stand for any secrets. They pushed forward to listen in. When my son Yehuda heard what she said, he burst out, "You drew God? You can't draw God!"

Ne'ema grabbed the picture and darted for her room, crying, "I can draw God if I want to!"

Now imagine that at age twenty-five Ne'ema continued to think that God is a purple-green guy-in-the-sky. Surely if someone were to ask her whether she believed in God, she would respond, "What? Of course not." She would probably consider herself an atheist. (One of my colleagues' standard response to an atheist is, "The God you don't believe in I don't believe in either.")

Most of us retain some sort of image of God from our childhood, and if we think for a moment, we might recall when the idea first registered on our juvenile consciousness. Many of us have been influenced by the Greek and Roman images of Zeus, others by Michelangelo's version in the Sistine Chapel, which looks every bit like old Zeus himself. It is no wonder that so many children (and adults too) imagine God as a powerful, aged man with a flowing white beard. Children need to give God a physical form, otherwise they cannot comprehend the idea. For them an invisible, incorporeal God is simply not there.

In a child's mind, according to his or her level of comprehension, God *has* to have a body, an imaginable form of some kind, to exist. But as the child grows up and matures intellectually and spiritually, he or she needs to find a new paradigm—a new framework for understanding God, for *seeing* God.

The problem is that most of us don't.

The Idol Smasher

Humanity has been struggling with this problem since the dawn of civilization. This was the genius and earthshaking contribution of Abraham. Four thousand years ago, he told a world that worshiped a panoply of idols representing every imaginable aspect of nature that there is only one unimaginable source of all creation. Can you imagine what a shock it must have been to hear that back then? God is imageless? How could that be?

The irony of it was that Abraham's father, Terach, was an idol-maker by profession. Jewish Oral Tradition tells us that as a child Abraham smashed all the idols in his father's shop. Responding to his father's fury, he boldly claimed that the biggest of the idols was responsible for the destruction. "But," countered his father, "he is just a statue; he can't do anything." And to that Abraham said simply, "Let your ears hear what your mouth has spoken."

God, who is responsible for the vastness and intricacy of creation, cannot be limited to any form, and especially not to an inanimate graven image. A mature and healthy soul must deny such childish imaginings.

As Rabbi Abraham Isaac Kook, great Kabbalist and philosopher living at the turn of the century, put it, "There is faith that is actually denial, and there is denial that is actually faith." When a person says that he believes in God, but in fact, the God he believes in is really a conceptual spiritual idol, an image of God that he has conjured up, then his faith is actually denial of truth, heresy. However, when a person professes atheism because he just can't believe in some almighty king with a white flowing beard floating somewhere in outer space, in a sense he is expressing true faith, because there is no such God.

The challenge is how to clean out such false imagery from one's mind—imagery that has grown thick, hard, and solid over time and, like a hard wall of cement blocks, is now presenting a very serious obstruction to really seeing God.

The place to start is with the big word: G-O-D.

Today people talk a great deal about God. It is fashionable to bring up spiritual matters at cocktail parties, but what are people really talking about when they say "God"?

A couple of years ago when a major publisher agreed to put out my last book, *Endless Light,* my editor, who was also the vice president of the company, said to me, "You know, Rabbi, quite frankly, five years ago we wouldn't even look at a book like this, a book about God. It would never sell. But today . . . what can I tell you? God is in."

It's a whole new age. God now sells. It's fashionable to believe in God. Not too long ago, it was not fashionable to believe in God. In fact, it was decidedly politically incorrect. Not so long ago, I remember a woman student, the head of a philosophy department at an important American college, who came to one of my seminars. She called herself a "closet believer." She actually believed in God, but she said that if she were to admit such a thing in academic circles she would be laughed out of the room and might even lose her job. Intelligent people simply didn't believe in God; faith was considered something primitive, passé, decidedly not academic. Therefore, she had to be a closet believer. Today, she can come out of the closet. How times have changed! But what concerns me about this trendiness of God is that trends come and go. Two hundred years ago God was fashionable—the founding fathers of America put God in the Declaration of Independence and "In God We Trust" on all American money. Fifty years ago, God was not fashionable—the founders of the State of Israel, after much argument, only cryptically referred to God as "Rock of Israel" when they wrote their Declaration of Independence. Now God is fashionable again.

BORDERS
BOOKS AND MUSIC
4745 ASHFORD-DUNWOODY RD
DUNWOODY GA 30338
(770) 396-0004

STORE: 0104 REG: 01/08 TRAN#: 7865
SALE 01/05/2002 EMP: 02007

SEEING GOD
6752967 QP T 12.00

	Subtotal	12.00
	GEORGIA 7% TAX	.84
1 Item	Total	12.84
	CASH	13.00
	CASH	.16-

01/05/2002 08:10PM

THANK YOU FOR SHOPPING AT BORDERS
PLEASE ASK ABOUT OUR SPECIAL EVENTS

Visit our website at www.borders.com!

exchanged for replacement copies of the original items only.

- Periodicals and newspapers may not be returned.
- Items purchased by check may be returned for cash after 10 business days.
- All returned checks will incur a $15 service charge.
- All other refunds will be granted in the form of the original payment.

BORDERS®

- Returns must be accompanied by the original receipt.
- Returns must be completed within 30 days.
- Merchandise must be in salable condition.
- Opened videos, discs and cassettes may be exchanged for replacement copies of the original items only.
- Periodicals and newspapers may not be returned.
- Items purchased by check may be returned for cash after 10 business days.
- All returned checks will incur a $15 service charge.
- All other refunds will be granted in the form of the original payment.

BORDERS®

- Returns must be accompanied by the original receipt.
- Returns must be completed within 30 days.
- Merchandise must be in salable condition.
- Opened videos, discs and cassettes may be exchanged for replacement copies of the original items only.
- Periodicals and newspapers may not be returned.
- Items purchased by check may be returned for cash after 10 business days.

To make sure that God isn't *just* fashionable and will not fall out of fashion next year along with platform shoes, we have to take great care. To make sure that God really becomes part of our lives and has a profound and healthy effect in improving the way we live and relate to each other, we have to pay attention to what we mean when we say "God."

The Death of God

Quite frankly, the word "God" does nothing for me. If anything, it interferes with my true faith. Personally, I don't believe in "God." It's an English word of German derivation and is not found in the Bible, if you read the Hebrew original. The word "God" has been so overused, abused, and misunderstood that it actually stands in the way of our discovering the ultimate truth we are seeking.

Thinking about this problem, I begin to understand what Nietzsche must have meant when he said God is dead. The concept of "God"—what we mean when we say "God"—*is* a dead concept. It is not real. The male, Zeus-like avenger floating about in heaven doesn't even come close to representing the reality.

How childish and counterproductive this concept is was brought home to me when one day, into my seminar walked a fellow wearing a T-shirt depicting an exchange from the Calvin and Hobbes comic strip. Hobbes, the toy tiger, is asking Calvin, the little boy, "Calvin, do you believe in God?" Calvin's reply is: "Well, *someone* is out to get me."

Unfortunately, many people harbor an image of God as some kind of almighty heavenly bully who is out to get them. No wonder they don't want to believe in that God; no wonder they don't have any idea how to connect with that God. As one woman said to me, "I just wish that He would leave me alone. I don't bother with Him;

He shouldn't bother with me." But down deep, such people really suffer from an intense fear of God and punishment. This is called theophobia. Often the people who suffer from theophobia describe themselves as atheists. They try to escape their mental torment by denying the God whom they actually continue to fear daily.

I understand their fears. I remember the first time I felt that kind of fear. I was a child watching *The Ten Commandments,* starring Charlton Heston as Moses. Only later on in my life did I realize what a negative experience that was for me. For one thing, the voice of God stayed imprinted on my consciousness for a very long time. Can you imagine the auditions for the part? Actors with a sweet, gentle voice need not apply! Only someone with a booming, loud, oppressive-sounding voice could be the voice of God.

These are the kinds of memories rambling around in most people's minds. In total they add up to an awful image of God. So, I believe that before real spiritual growth is possible we must get rid of God.

Just like Abraham, we need to smash our own graven images, free ourselves from the conceptual idolatry obstructing the eyes of our soul. The time has come to see the One whom we seek.

The One Who Was, Is, and Will Be

The name in the Bible that unfortunately has been translated as "God" is comprised of the Hebrew letters *yud, hey, vav, hey* and is written out in English as "Y/H/V/H." It is important to know that "Y/H/V/H" is not a word at all, but a tetragrammaton—*the* tetragrammaton as there is only one—standing for "was/is/and/will be." The tetragrammaton condenses the three Hebrew forms of the verb "to be" suggesting the timeless source and context of all being.

Jewish law prohibits the pronunciation of the tetragrammaton, and therefore in prayer, religious Jews substitute a completely different word—*Adonai* (meaning "Lord")—when they come to "Y/H/V/H."

How very strange to see a word and say something else. Of course, this is done to remind the worshiper that what he/she sees cannot be said, what he/she experiences cannot really be captured in words or concepts. The sages of old, in their vast wisdom, understood that people love the crutch of images and therefore need constant reminders to humbly accept the limitations of their conceptual minds. How can a human mind grasp Y/H/V/H? How can the human mind imagine the Ultimate Timeless Reality?

This is a very difficult idea to grasp because it surpasses our minds. It's like a drop of water in the ocean, trying to grasp the ocean. Indeed, the best we can say is that we each embody an aspect of reality, but we are not reality. Like the drop of water in the ocean, we exist within reality. Because reality is Y/H/V/H.

When Jews celebrate Passover, they sing a song from the Haggadah: "Blessed Is the Place." One of the terms used to describe Y/H/V/H is the "Place." Why the "Place"? Because it suggests Y/H/V/H is the place in which we exist, is the reality within which we exist.

If you believe in the Big Bang theory—that the world came into being as a primordial explosion with masses of hot, whirling gases that eventually condensed into stars and planets—you would still have to ask: Where did all this happen? What place was this in which the explosion took place? Who facilitated this event?

The answer is Y/H/V/H, the Ultimate Reality—the One who embraces all time, all space and all beings.

The Kabbalah warns that we should not affix any name or letter to the Ultimate Reality. (The Kabbalah refers to the Ultimate Reality as *Ein Sof*—the Endless One.) We can't stuff something as vast and abstract as that into any rigid concept or image. Even the tetragrammaton is at best only a hint, because the One to whom it refers is beyond names and concepts.

So what are we to do when trying to speak of Y/H/V/H without getting stuck in the dead concept that we are trying to get rid of? The Jewish answer is to avoid the problem by simply saying *Hashem,* which in Hebrew simply means "the name." This helps one avoid becoming too familiar with a name, indeed it avoids using a name. Saying "the name"—Hashem—reminds us that the Ultimate Reality is in fact beyond all names, all terms, all images. When we say Hashem, we realize that we only possess a simplistic, limited, inadequate understanding of the Ultimate Reality, the Source of All Being, the Place or the Context of All That Exists.

We don't—indeed, we can't—have an understanding of Hashem, but we can and do have a relationship with Hashem.

God is dead; it is a lifeless concept, a dead word. But Hashem is alive, the Ultimate *Living* Reality.

My friend Ron told me a story about how he got rid of God and discovered Hashem. He was at the Western Wall in Jerusalem, the last remnant of the Holy Temple, which stood over two thousand years ago, and even though he always considered himself an atheist, he thought, What the heck, here I am at the Wall, I should do something spiritual. So he turned to a religious fellow next to him and asked, "Well, what does one do here?"

The fellow responded, "Why don't you recite some psalms?" And he handed him a book of psalms. Ron thought that seemed appropriate and he began to read some verses. Sure enough just within the first few words he hit upon the "God" word. Although he felt annoyed, he decided to continue. But again the "God" word appeared. Now he was getting very frustrated. How can I say this if I don't believe in God? he asked himself. Do I have to believe in God to have a spiritual experience?

Since Ron is a computer engineer, he decided to relate to his predicament as if it were a computer problem. When there is computer data that he can't use, he creates a buffer zone and puts it there. Ron decided, I'll put the "God" word in a mental buffer zone and simply disregard it so I can continue reading the psalms without getting aggravated. And that's what he did.

Ron then continued reading and suddenly felt overwhelmed by a flood of inspiration released by the moving poetic words of King David. He told me that he was struck by a profound spiritual experience, which he had never felt before. It was as if he were surrounded by light. This was the beginning of Ron's belief in Hashem. Only when he got rid of "God" was he able to see Hashem.

Paradigm Shift

It is interesting to note that Nietzsche, besides proclaiming that God is dead, also said that unless we experience an infinite whole working through us, our lives have no meaning. Nietzsche didn't believe in "God." And neither do I. I believe in the Infinite Whole, the One who was, is, and always will be—Hashem.

Relating to Hashem requires a total paradigm shift for most people. The general way people understand God is that there's reality, and then there's God *in* reality. Within that reality God has created little you and me. And so here we are in reality, standing alongside Almighty God. With that picture before our eyes, we cannot help but feeling very small, insignificant, threatened. Everything—all creation and we along with it—looks so puny and petty compared to God. That's why we shirk away from that God and deny His existence. We simply cannot deal with the comparison, with feeling like nothing next to God.

People have this image of a God floating somewhere in reality, who for some reason decided to create you and me. Yet that perfect being floating in reality created a bunch of imperfect beings. We can't help but always compare ourselves to this almighty perfect being. We can't help but always feel like nothing next to this almighty perfect being. We then ask, "Do we have to surrender to God, and just religiously accept the ideology that we are nothing?" Certain religious paths would answer, "Yes, we are nothing, and this world is nothing. And that is the highest realization to strive for—personal annihilation."

However, for those of us who are not willing to believe that we are nothing, the alternative approach is the flip side of the coin—God is nothing—because in order to believe in myself I can't believe in God.

The paradigm that imagines a God *in* reality either leads to a philosophy of absolute surrender, total effacement of the human being and life in this world, or—for those not willing to accept that—it leads to atheism. By the way, the atheist, by denying God, is actually partly right—*in* reality there is no God.

But the Kabbalah inspires a complete paradigm shift. It teaches that Hashem does not exist in reality—Hashem is reality. And we do not exist alongside Hashem, we exist within Hashem, within the reality that is Hashem.

Hashem is the place. Indeed, Hashem is the all-embracing context for everything. So there can't be you and God standing side by side in reality. There is only one reality that is Hashem, and you exist in Hashem.

You exist within reality, embody an aspect of reality, participate in reality. That's a completely different understanding. All of a sudden, you are no longer a puny insignificant creature existing alongside God, sharing the same place. In light of this perspective, you are not only not puny, not insignificant, not nothing, your existence is intensified because it is a manifestation of the Divine.

Seeing God is all about getting in touch with reality.

Personal God

When I talk about reality in my seminars, sometimes my students object. They complain that "reality" sounds too impersonal. "What happened to the personal God?" they ask.

But the Ultimate Reality, Hashem, Y/H/V/H, is not impersonal. This reality embraces you and me and is the source of and context for you and me, therefore, Hashem couldn't be any less personal than you and me. In fact, Hashem is infinitely more personal. People think that reality is dead empty space, but reality is actually conscious, alive, and loving. Therefore, we cannot speak of reality in an impersonal way. We can't ask, for example, "What is reality?" We must ask, "Who is reality? Who is the source of all consciousness? Who is the source of all life? Who is the source of love? Who accommodates everything we see in this world?"

The answer is Hashem.

This is expressed by Rabbi Moshe Cordovero, who was a great Kabbalist living in the sixteenth century, "Hashem is found in all things. All things are found in Hashem. There is nothing devoid of Hashem's Divinity. Everything is in Hashem. Hashem is in everything, beyond everything."

It is important for me to clarify that this is not a statement of pantheism. Pantheism is a theory that all is God. That is not what Rabbi Cordovero means, and it is not what I am trying to get across.

Pantheism depends on the equation: God equals universe. Deduct the universe and God becomes nothing. But Judaism holds that Hashem existed before the universe and in fact created the universe, and if the universe ceases to exist, Hashem will continue to exist just as whole without it. That idea is called panentheism, which means that all is included within Hashem. A dramatically different concept from pantheism. All is included within the Divine, but if I did not exist and you did not exist, Hashem wouldn't be diminished.

One metaphor that can be helpful for understanding our relationship to Hashem is the relationship between the thought and the thinker. If I create a man in my mind, where does that man exist? In my mind. That man exists within me, yet I'm not that man. That man is not me. He continues to exist as long as I continue to think him. If I stop thinking about him, he ceases to exist but I am no less who I was before I created him in my imagination.

Similarly, we are the product of Hashem's creation. We exist in Hashem. But we are not Hashem and Hashem is not us. It's a mystical idea. There is nothing devoid of Hashem. Everything is in Hashem, Hashem is in everything, but Hashem is *beyond* everything.

We exist within reality, we embody reality, and yet we are not reality. And if we would cease to exist, reality would continue on, no less than before or after our creation.

When I tried to explain this to my seven-year-old son, it went like this:

"Nuri, where is Hashem?"

"He's over there," he answers, confidently pointing to the sky. "In heaven."

"No. Hashem isn't over there, Hashem is everywhere."

"Oh."

"Now, where are you and I?"

"Well," he was more cautious now, expecting something tricky within the question. "We're over here."

"No," I said, "You and I are actually within Hashem. Do you understand that? Hashem isn't over there, and you and I are not over here. Hashem is everywhere and we're in Hashem."

My son thought about this for a few moments, trying to understand it. Then he exclaimed, "I got it! I got it! Wow! Hashem is so fat!"

Somehow he had to make a picture of Hashem, fat enough to encompass two other people, because a child's mind cannot deal in abstractions. That's why if a third grader is having trouble figuring out how much is fourteen minus nine, you tell him, "If you have fourteen candies, and you give away nine to your sister, how many candies will you have left?" He'll get it right away. He'll see the candies disappearing in his mind. But as he matures, he is expected to let go of childish, limited concrete concepts. He can't be thinking of candy each time he adds or subtracts, nor can he be thinking of a fat balloon each time he thinks of God.

If we want an adult relationship with Hashem, then we must be willing to change the paradigm. Letting go of old concepts, however, is extremely difficult. The human mind can be like a prison and getting out of the prison of our imagination is sometimes more difficult than getting out of a prison made of stones and bars. If we become prisoners to the unhealthy concept of God, then we view all of life through a framework of God versus me. And no wonder religion turns us off.

When we read that an omnipotent being over there gave us this or that commandment, we say in our childish minds, Oh yeah? So what? It becomes a question of who is going to win. Are we going to surrender to that being over there?

But, if we can make the jump from counting candies to the abstractions of algebra, we can also succeed in freeing our minds from unhealthy stilted images of God. Only when we remove from our mind's eyes those blindfolds of dead concepts can we begin to open the eyes of the soul and see in a new way. But once we do, we also open up the possibility of truly seeing Hashem.

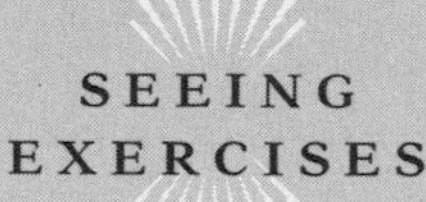

SEEING EXERCISES

1. Try to recall who God was for you when you were a child.
2. Using your nondominant hand, write a letter to God starting with one of the following:

   Dear God,
   I always wanted to ask You . . .
   Dear God,
   I feel you close to me when . . .
   Dear God,
   This is my only request to you.

3. List key concepts you learned about God when you were growing up. What or who was the source for your information—parents, friends, TV, religious instruction?
4. Take one minute and write any word association that you now have with the word "God." Try not to think, just write whatever comes to your mind.
5. Can you remember a time when you felt jealous, angry, or resentful toward God?
6. Can you take those events and reframe them into more positive feelings and meaningful lessons?

two

SPIRITUAL SEEING

Opening the eyes of the soul to see Hashem doesn't happen just like that, even once the blindfolds are gone. Like a person who has been in a dark room for a long time and then comes out into strong sunlight, you need time to adjust and refocus.

So it takes some patience to prepare and adjust and learn totally new ways of seeing.

Back in the early 1970s a great many experiments were done in the field of childhood development and learning. One discovery was that children can learn in dramatic new ways if not imprinted by an educational system. So, for example, if a child went to school and learned addition and multiplication, then that child would forever think in a linear way—one plus one equals two plus one equals three. When such a child was presented with a page full of dots, the only way he or she could tell that there were eighty-eight dots on the page was by either counting them one by one or by counting the horizontal and vertical rows and then multiplying the two. However, a child who was never imprinted with linear thinking could simply look at the page of dots holistically, so to speak, and instantly say: "Eighty-eight."

That is the kind of approach we need in order to see Hashem. We need to learn a new way—seeing allness. What does it mean to see "allness"?

Rabbi Abraham Isaac Kook, in his classic work, *The Lights of Holiness,* contrasts spiritual seeing with nonspiritual seeing, which he calls secular seeing. "Spiritual seeing" is a way of seeing holistically, where a person sees the whole rather than the separate details. It's focusing on the total picture, the allness.

"Secular seeing," as Rabbi Kook defines it, is just the opposite. In fact, in Hebrew, the word *hiloni,* meaning secular, comes from the word *hol,* meaning sand.

Just as sand is made up of small, separate granules, so secular seeing is a way of seeing the world as made up of small, separate components.

It is like the difference between seeing with a wide-angle lens and with a zoom lens. If your camera zooms in on my freckle, suddenly this freckle, a very tiny part of me, fills the entire viewfinder. Without the benefit of wide-angle perspective, you can see a freckle and think that it is a huge blemish.

A wide-angle lens, on the other hand, shows you the whole face, the whole body. In that context, from the broad perspective, the freckle is hardly noticeable; it's nothing more than one spot of pigment, part of a multibillion universe of the cells of my body.

The broader your perspective, the more of Hashem you will see in your life. But if you have narrow tunnel vision, then you will see less of Hashem.

The ideal way of seeing, the ultimate in spiritual seeing, is to see with the broadest field of vision possible—everything at the same time. Unfortunately, we are not likely to achieve that as long as we are bound by the limitations of this dimension. So, for our purposes, we will be aiming to see as much of the whole as possible rather than the fragments or the details.

I must note here that I am by no means suggesting that details are not important. Indeed, they are very important. And once you become sensitive to seeing allness, then the details become intensified, because you see the details within the context of the whole reality. And the whole reality is Hashem.

The wider your vision, the broader your mind, the more you are able to actually see reality. And the more you can see reality, the more you are able to see and welcome Hashem into your life.

This is a very important principle. Kabbalah tells us that what you see is what you get. In other words, the more you are aware of allness, the more allness can pour into your life. If you don't see or acknowledge it, then it's really not going to be there for you.

Learning to See Allness

One day I was walking into the center of Jerusalem, the usual route I take along Jaffa Road, and I suddenly realized that when I walk, I keep my head down. I asked myself, Why don't you look up? So, at that moment I did, and I saw a completely new and different Jaffa Road. I used to think that Jaffa Road was stores and tree trunks. I didn't know that there are incredible canopies of leaves above, and fountains of palm fronds jutting into the sky, and birds flying to and from, singing sweetly, and colorful window boxes with cascading flowers, and beautiful architectural details to the multistory buildings—arched windows, ornate balconies adorned with filigree ironwork, emblems sculpted in stone. All of a sudden I saw a whole new world just because I had looked up and expanded my vision for a moment.

The world you see is a function of how narrow your view is. Just for a moment, look at the room you are sitting in. Rather than focusing on anything in particular, try to see it with the fullness of vision: the ceiling, the floor, the corners of the room, all four walls. Do you perceive a different room?

Now, if you could just transfer that fullness of vision to everything you see and do, then you'd be living in a different world. And that world might give you a taste of what the Garden of Eden must have been like.

It should not surprise us to learn then that the first man and woman were in the Garden of Eden *because* they were able to see allness. They felt one with Hashem, one with all of creation. But when they ate from the forbidden Tree of Knowledge, they damaged the breadth of their spiritual vision. As a result of that damage, their perspective became so skewed that they could only see a very narrow slice of reality, which they perceived as the physical world. Indeed, as a result of their change of perspective, they even experienced themselves as physical.

The Jewish Oral Tradition, the Midrash, tells us that in the Garden of Eden, Adam and Eve didn't have bodies of skin, they had bodies of "light." The Midrash also states that everything in the Garden of Eden had that same quality: "There were no shadows in the Garden of Eden." In other words, nothing was opaque or heavy or dark or solid—the way we experience matter today. There was a luminescence to everything.

The difference was all in how Adam and Eve saw and experienced their world. Their bodies, the trees, the animals, the birds were translucent so that through the tree you could see the bird, so that the bird appeared to be inside the tree, and through the bird, the elephant, so that the elephant appeared part of the bird and of the tree, and through the elephant, a horse . . . and man and woman and fish and water and sky. Nothing obscured anything else and it all appeared part of the same beautiful whole.

It's only after Adam and Eve ate of the forbidden tree—when they partook of the knowledge of good and evil—that they experienced themselves as heavy and opaque. Suddenly, they saw that they had bodies of flesh, and they experienced themselves as garbed in a sack of skin that created a boundary between them and the rest of creation.

When they experienced themselves as having bodies of light, there was no sense of separation between themselves and the rest of reality. Their entire self-definition was bound up with allness. They didn't know it could be any different.

The snake was the one to tell them that it could be different—it could be better. The picture the snake painted for them in the famous story went something like this: "Hey, Eve, come have a bite. . . . Hashem doesn't want you to eat from this special tree because He is afraid that if you eat from it, you'll be just like Him." Then the snake went into his best line: "You know why He is doing it, don't you? He wants to be the only one who is independent and powerful. He wants to be the only god—He doesn't want competition. So, He's keeping you down, subordinate, inferior. But if you eat from this tree, you'll see things in a whole new way."

That was the lie of the snake—presenting Hashem and humanity as separate conflicting entities.

Once Eve, and later Adam, bought into this lie, into this illusion of separateness and independence, they began to have exactly that experience. Be careful what you wish for, it might come true, the saying goes. That is exactly what happened to them. They suddenly experienced their bodies as physical—opaque, solid, heavy. The physical body of the human being was born out of the first humans' mistaken attitude that to be separate and independent would somehow be better.

Children of the Lie

As the children of Adam and Eve, we experience ourselves as isolated, independent, self-defined entities, separate from the whole reality in which we truly find our beings. This lonely experience is the snake's lie, and the source of much of the pain and evil in this world.

The Kabbalah describes the force of evil as the *sitra aher,* meaning "the other side," and its basic message is that we are on one side and Hashem is on the other. But once we come to recognize this powerful illusion as false, we quickly see that Hashem is always and only on our side. There are no two sides, only oneness and wholeness.

The physical world appears dense and opaque because we see reality from such a narrow perspective. We are seeing only a partial picture, a fragment of reality out of the context of the Ultimate Reality that is Hashem.

We see details out of context and mistakenly think they are the whole picture. Because of the narrowness of our vision, everything appears hard, solid—each object distinct, separate, unrelated. Physicists tell us that that is not accurate at all. Our world is really composed of energy. Even something as seemingly solid as a rock is a swarming hive of protons and electrons that only appear stationary because of their density. But what's even more fascinating is that the rock and the bird are made up of the same elements in different combination. If we could see through superbionic eyes, we'd see the dance of energy within and between each object of creation.

Perhaps Vincent van Gogh caught a glimpse of this when he painted his *Starry Night;* his stars are not points of light in the sky, but swirls of energy, and as the Hubble Space Telescope has demonstrated, this *is* what stars really are.

But most of the time the narrowness of our vision prevents us from seeing the dance of energy and the oneness that permeates all. We seem to exist in a different world from the one that is the true reality. What is it that creates this illusion? The Kabbalah says that it is our attitude of separateness that creates for us a world of *klipot,* literally of "hard shells." We become encased in hard shells that separate us from Hashem.

It may surprise you to hear that the Kabbalah teaches that in the future we're going to realize that we have been in the Garden of Eden all along. We feel like we left it because we closed our souls' eyes to it. It's as if we entered a dark, hard, cold cave, thinking that this "hard shell" would protect us. We are choosing to live in the world of hard boundaries, instead of the world of *oneness.* By narrowing our vision, we entered this self-imposed prison of perception. We really continue to exist within the Ultimate Reality, we just don't experience life that way.

Seeing Big, Seeing Small

Did you ever see a picture taken from a newspaper and magnified many times over? Enlarged, the picture appears as if made up of separate, unrelated dots, and if the magnification is high enough, you can actually lose the ability to see the picture, because the dots dominate your field of vision. Looking at the dots, instead of the picture is a kind of visual myopia that the Kabbalah calls *mohin de katnut* or "narrow mindedness." When you are in a state of *mohin de katnut,* then the world you live in is a narrow slice of reality and everything is fragmented and disconnected. You are focusing on the dots, not on the picture.

But there is another way of seeing. The Kabbalah refers to it as *mohin de gadlut,* broad-mindedness. An open mind sees a broader view and gets the total picture.

The ultimate in *mohin de gadlut* is to be able to look at your life, at this world, and at history from the broadest possible perspective. Then you have the capacity to understand it all in a complete and united way.

There is an amusing story told about a Jurassic man who visits the garment district in New York. He sees a tailor unrolling a beautiful bolt of cloth and cutting it into pieces. "These modern people are crazy," he mumbles to himself. "Destroying a beautiful cloth in that way."

A few days later, he finds himself in the same place and now he sees a customer putting on a suit made of the beautiful cloth. Not only has it not been destroyed, it is better, because now it is a beautiful, useful, complete garment.

That is the difference between small-mindedness and broad-mindedness. Small-mindedness sees destruction, cut-up pieces; broad-mindedness sees a beautiful garment in the making.

The broader, more expanded our minds are, the more we see reality, the more we are able to see Hashem. And the more we are able to see Hashem, the more Hashem is in our world and in our lives. It's a completely different level of consciousness. You see the details of life—you even see more details that you might ordinarily—but you see them clearly related and united in context.

Then every detail of reality becomes important. Details *by them-*

selves are not important. But when you experience these details *within* the greater context, then each detail is intensified by its relation to that greater context. And that is when you actually begin to get a glimpse of Hashem—the All in Everything.

The saying goes, God is in the details, but that is true only after you have seen the details within God.

Eyes of Wonder

Thus far we've established that to see Hashem, we must learn to see allness. We've discussed what "allness" means, but we haven't discussed how this can happen.

To see allness, you need eyes of wonder.

"Eyes of wonder" are eyes of innocence, eyes not jaded and obscured by preconceptions and notions that have nothing to do with the reality of what exists.

Most adults have forgotten the state of awareness called wonder. We have to relearn it from innocents—babies, toddlers, our children—before they have been contaminated by the anthropomorphic notions that adults feed them. When they are still innocent, children can teach us how to see Hashem. They see Hashem more than we do.

In fact, it's been said that in ages past a prophet had to be an adult child. A prophet was an adult who had evolved intellectually and yet had not lost the sensitivity and surprise and amazement that a child constantly experiences.

I get a great kick watching my children watch the world. My baby looks at each object as if he's never seen it before. He is so surprised by it. He can sit there and look at his hand for the longest time as if it's the most fascinating object. And he just giggles and laughs.

What is it that children see? Once I was walking down the street with my two-year-old son. He looked up and saw something fly by in the sky. He was just beginning to talk, so he said in his limited Hebrew, *"Abba, ze,"* meaning, "Daddy, that."

I looked up, and replied, "Oh, that's a bird."

My son repeated, "Bird."

I felt really good; I'm an adult teaching him how to see the world and how to say the word "bird."

Then, all of a sudden, another bird went flying by. My son said "Oh, *Abba, ze."*

I replied, "That's also a bird."

I could see in my son's eyes the confusion. How could they both be birds? They were so different.

You see what happens—we get used to experiencing reality by labeling everything. We cease seeing this amazing, unique, flying creature; we just slap an easy label onto it—"bird." We become existential file clerks. We don't care what the document says, we just care about where to file it. That creature goes under "bird." Finished. We stop seeing the indescribable "that."

The Kaballah tells us that at certain times in the Torah the term "That" alludes to Hashem. The goal is to be able to see "That" without labels, without preconceptions. Labels prevent us from directly experiencing reality; they obliterate our vision, and prevent us from seeing Hashem.

We have to train ourselves to see that which is without defining or comparing it to anything else.

Children have that capacity. They see pure uniqueness. We have come up with so many precise labels and definitions that we think we know whatever it is we are encountering. But children know better. They know that they don't know what it is. And that openness allows them to really see what they are looking at.

Children see something and they are struck with awe. What does it mean to be struck with awe? It's a little like seeing fireworks. When we see fireworks, we exclaim, "Ohhhhhhh," "Ahhhhhhh." We're so dazzled, we simply have no words.

That moment when you see a waterfall, or a rainbow, or a stormy sea, or a newborn baby, and you are overwhelmed with feelings of reverence and wonder, when you are so struck with amazement at Hashem's brilliance and genius that you can only utter, "Ahhhhh," that is awe. And it is the beginning of seeing Hashem. It is the beginning of seeing reality, of seeing what is real rather than looking at the world through a filter of interpretations and categorizations. That is the beginning of seeing allness through the eyes of wonder.

This is, of course, where Adam and Eve went wrong. By eating from the forbidden Tree of the Knowledge of Good and Evil, they acquired a set of definitions and labels that broke their vision of allness into separate pieces.

It is not that Hashem didn't want them to have knowledge—that is not why the tree was off limits—it's just that Hashem wanted them first to see allness through the eyes of wonder.

They saw allness, but they took it for granted. They didn't marvel at it. They didn't yet see the wonder in it that they needed to experience. But they short-circuited the plan by eating from the tree. They never enjoyed seeing allness with the eyes of wonder without the interference of knowledge, words, and ideas. The Kabbalah explains that Hashem had every intention of giving the first man and woman the opportunity to eat from the tree. But not before wonder.

The Obstacle of Knowledge

First we have to see the world without knowledge, without expectations, without the demand that the world fit into our ideas and definitions. Just see it. Once we have experienced seeing it, knowledge will be a helpful although limited tool for communicating what we have seen, but we'll never allow it to interfere with what we understood before the labels and categories.

The Talmud recommends that before we pray, we should sit in silence, that we should meditate for a certain amount of time. This is because if we seek to know Hashem in silence, without words, without concepts, then we will be able to address Hashem with sincerity and honesty, without confusing our words with the truth of Hashem, Who is beyond words.

But you may be asking: "What is so wrong with words?" After all the world was created with words. God's law—the Torah—is made up of words. We are commanded to speak certain words—pronounce blessings—before undertaking many simple actions, like eating and drinking. If anything, words sanctify actions.

To understand when words are appropriate and when they interfere, we need to take a look at the three Hebrew words that are translated as "word" in English. They are: *mila, teva,* and *davar.* If we understand their derivative meanings, we will understand the Talmud's attitude toward words, and toward language in general.

Mila, for example, is also used to refer to the rite of circumcision, which is called *brit mila—mila* literally means "cut." It is an appropriate word for circumcisions, but why does it also mean "word"? Because words have the capacity to cut reality into pieces. That's the problem. I can't see reality through words because words fragment reality. I no longer see allness. I see just my carefully labeled pieces.

The second word *teva* literally means "box." And that's another negative aspect of words—they put reality into boxes. They cut that reality into pieces and pigeonhole each one: tree, cloud, bird, sky, ocean, and so on.

The third word *davar* means "thing." It suggests that words have the capacity of taking reality and turning it into a bunch of things—inanimate, distinct objects.

King David, who so beautifully used words in composing his psalms, also wrote: "Silence is His praise." Was King David saying that he was wrong to use words to praise Hashem? I don't think so. But King David understood that only a person who *first* knows Hashem in silence, only a person who sees *before* speaking, can utter words of praise that do not interfere with his vision. But what unfortunately happens is that our words and concepts obstruct our seeing whole.

Perhaps that is why for the first two years of life, a child experiences a world without really understanding words and without the ability to speak. Childhood is a time for wonder. Adam and Eve had to spend a little time in wonder before they started using knowledge to define, evaluate, and clarify. Words are great, but if they substitute for wonder, or if they are introduced prematurely, then we lose our direct encounter with reality.

We have to give some time to the development of the right brain—the source of intuition and feeling—before we kick in with the left brain, which formulates, articulates, and verbalizes. So, silence is the necessary prerequisite to seeing and then praising Hashem.

Silence Is Golden

The Talmud teaches that "silence is a protective fence to wisdom." To guard our true wisdom we need to get in touch with what we know in silence before we try to put it into limited words.

There is a Midrashic tale that when a baby is still in the womb, an angel comes and teaches it all of wisdom. But just before the baby is born, the angel touches the baby above the lip—causing the little crevice there—and the baby forgets all it had learned. Clearly the Midrash means to communicate the message that knowledge is innate and that education is not a process of discovery but of recovery.

But what is the message behind the odd action of the angel. To cause forgetfulness, wouldn't it make more sense to tap the baby on the head rather than the mouth?

When we come into this world with the desire to speak, we already forget the essence of what we really know, which is before words and beyond words. The essence of truth cannot be put into words. There is a level of knowing that transcends words.

As babies we have the capacity of seeing allness in everything, but once we are born into this world, with the need to put what we see into words, we fragment that vision. The greatest obstacle to seeing Hashem with eyes of wonder is our conviction that we have to label and categorize what we see.

When we rely on assumptions, mental clichés, and we project our labels, our notions, our pictures onto reality, we cut off all possibility of experiencing reality, of seeing Hashem. We see what we have programmed ourselves to see, rather than seeing reality as it is. And we are so sure that our interpretation is reality.

I learned this lesson one day when I decided to have my handwriting analyzed. I was sitting in the waiting room, filling out the application, which called for the drawing of a tree on one page. There were other people there, and I couldn't help but peek over at what they were doing. The fellow next to me was drawing a huge tree in the middle of the page, but the fellow next to him drew a little tree over in the corner. Mr. Big Tree looked over and happened to notice what Mr. Little Tree was doing. I could see that Mr. Big Tree was dying to say something, but he hesitated. Finally he tapped

Mr. Little Tree on the shoulder and said, very politely, "Excuse me, but you're not filling out the application right."

Mr. Little Tree replied, "Oh no, what am I doing wrong?"

Mr. Big Tree asked, "Your tree."

"The application said to draw a tree."

"Yes, but see what it says? 'Draw a tree on this page.' That means the whole page not the corner. And besides, what you're drawing is not a tree, but a shrub. You're supposed to draw a tree like mine."

So Mr. Little Tree looked over at Mr. Big Tree's big tree, and he uttered an "Aah" of understanding. He rubbed out his little tree and started drawing a big tree in the center of the page.

All the application really said was to draw a tree. But Mr. Big Tree immediately understood that to mean on the full page, and he assumed that his interpretation was reality, rather than his interpretation of reality.

Our assumptions are the greatest obstacles to seeing reality. We are stuck in our interpretations of it, and we assume that our way of seeing it is the way it truly is. And rather than seeing the allness, we shrink it down to our level and see instead a narrow slice of allness rather than what it really is—everything.

Betty Edwards, the author of *Drawing on the Right Side of the Brain,* was an art teacher who couldn't understand why her students had difficulty copying pictures. So, on a hunch, she asked them to turn the picture they were copying upside down. Now, when they copied the picture, the results were amazingly accurate. At first, she couldn't understand why, when the tree was right side up, the students had difficulty copying it, but when they turned it around, they drew it accurately. Then she formulated a theory, which she explains in her book.

She says that when you look at a picture, your left brain, which is very verbal, identifies it—for example, a tree. So you start drawing a tree. But you are not drawing a tree that's in the picture, because you are not able to see that picture anymore. Your left brain has substituted a file image, your previously formulated, preconceived notion of a tree. And that is the image you are trying to copy, not the one in front of your eyes. But when you fool the left brain—when you turn the picture upside down so the left brain can't immediately categorize what it is seeing—then you are free to see what is really there.

When the left brain doesn't have a word for it, it can't flash an image in your head, and then the right brain, which is holistic, experiential, is free to have a direct encounter with the picture and to draw it as it is.

This is an amazing insight. Betty Edwards's theory helps us understand what it means to see reality, rather than our picture of reality. As long as we have a whole filing system of concepts, we live inside our concepts, rather than in reality.

When I was in high school, I went with a couple of friends to a hip café in downtown Toronto. The café had live folk music, so we went to hear the musicians. There we were, sitting at a table, trying to decide what to order. When the waitress came, I was still engrossed in looking at the menu. Finally, I looked up to order, and I shrieked, "Mrs. Hobbs!" I couldn't believe my eyes—it was Mrs. Hobbs, my math teacher. I had seen her just that day in math class. The shock of seeing her in this totally different context dumbfounded me.

Incredulous, I asked her, "What are you doing here?"

"I'm a waitress," she replied simply.

"How can you be a waitress? You can't be a waitress," I stammered. "You're a math teacher."

"In fact, not only am I a waitress," she answered, "but I own this café."

"What?" I was stunned. "What are you doing teaching math?"

"I like it."

This was too much for my head. Mrs. Hobbs was a math teacher; to me, she didn't exist outside the classroom. But here I find out that she and her family own a café, that she is a waitress—and not only that, she is also somebody's daughter and somebody's wife, and a mother, and probably an aunt, and a friend, and a host of other things.

But the real truth is, she is none of these things. She is not a daughter, she's not a mother, she's not a math teacher. She is a unique expression of reality, created in the image of Hashem. But I'm locked into my filing cabinet. My labels have become my blindfold to seeing what is real. I see only my concepts of what is, rather than what truly is.

Seeing What Truly Is

The greatest obstacle to seeing Hashem is our filing cabinet of labels and preconceptions. Our filing cabinet gives us a sense of being in control. When an experience comes along, we know right where to put it. When we say that we understand something, we mean that we know which file to stuff it into. But true understanding is knowing that there are things beyond our comprehension, and when you begin to discover the incomprehensible, you discover Hashem.

This realization hit me like a ton of bricks at the birth of my first child. My wife, Chana, and I did all the birthing prep courses and read all the books we could get our hands on. But when that baby came into the world, I was literally in total shock. Even after all the knowledge I had accumulated I was completely taken by surprise. It was clear to me that even seeing is not believing. Only then I discovered that Hashem becomes believable only when life becomes unbelievable.

One day my son Anani asked me how is it that when it is day for us in Israel, it is night for Grandpa and Grandma in Canada? I took a tennis ball and a basketball to demonstrate how the earth (the tennis ball) rotates on its axis and circles the sun (the basketball). As I explained this simple concept, feeling delighted to share this very basic knowledge with my son, I saw the incredulous look on his face.

Suddenly I got a glimpse of how all this looked to my son's pure eyes of wonder. I then realized how utterly arrogant it was of me to think that I could actually explain the movement of the universe. My son's expression communicated to me how unbelievable it all was. It's not so simple—this tennis ball moves around this basketball—it's incredibly mysterious and complex. Think of it, the earth is a mass of rock and soil, eight thousand miles in diameter, covered with an envelope of gases and with a hot liquid inner core. It is 93 million miles from the sun, which is really a star, a self-luminous body of exploding nuclear reactions that is 865,400 miles in diameter. These giants are spinning out in space in a precise order and rhythm we are just barely beginning to understand. When that came to me, at that moment, I got a glimpse of Hashem.

If it had not been for my son's incredulous face I would have continued to think of the sun and earth as two balls out in space—a model I had seen in science class. I would have had before my eyes an image that was as far away from the reality as the earth is from the sun.

The Gift of the Unexpected

One obstacle to seeing reality is our resistance to the new and unexpected, to the innovations that do not fit into our old, cherished concepts. We don't know how to look at things with totally fresh eyes of wonder.

There is a wonderful parable about a dove that illustrates the danger of forcing everything new into our existing concepts. It says that originally doves had no wings. One poor dove was being constantly harassed by a lion. Every day the lion would run after the dove, and the dove would just barely escape.

One day the dove prayed to Hashem: "Hashem, I'm a little dove. I can't outrun this lion every day. One of these days he's going to catch me. I need help. Please, Hashem, help me."

Sure enough, Hashem answered this dove's prayers. The dove woke up the next morning and found she had wings. "Wow! Check these things out! Terrific!" With these wings she would get away from the lion; now she was feeling really confident and safe. As soon as she saw the lion, she called out to him, "Hey, here I am! Ha, ha, I'm over here." She stood there jauntily, figuring that she would wait until the lion got very close so she could show him what she could now do with wings. The lion charged after the dove, and when he was inches from her, the dove started running away.

But something strange happened. The dove tripped over her new wings. Instead of helping her run faster, the wings got in her way. The lion was on top of her now, and before she could pick herself up . . . well, it's a sad story.

When the dove got to bird heaven, she complained to Hashem, "I'm a little dove. The lion was harassing me. I prayed to you to help me, and you gave me wings. But instead of the wings helping me to run faster, they interfered with my speed."

Hashem responded: "You foolish dove. I didn't give you those wings to run with. I gave you those wings to fly with."

The dove was too fixated in her perspective to see that the wings could have opened her up to a completely new experience. She was just expecting to run faster.

We need to be willing to see things in a whole new way. That's what geniuses are all about. A genius is not stuck in somebody else's mental clichés, in the conventional notions of the world. The genius says, "I want to see it like I've never seen it before." He or she questions the way everybody else understands it. Who says the world is flat? Who says that time is absolute?

Many great scientific discoveries occur in this way. A scientist sets out to prove his theory. He conducts experiments that he expects will prove him right. But often the results indicate something totally unexpected. At that point, many scientists throw away the experiment rather than their belief systems. But the truly great ones, the geniuses among them, reformulate their concepts of reality according to the data. That's how all the great paradigm shifts in scientific history come about. That is spiritual seeing: seeing what is, rather than your concept of what is.

This, of course, was the genius of Abraham. To the mind of the world of his day, when it was obvious and accepted that idols had meaning, he was a maladjusted person. But Abraham saw in a whole new way. Imagine the courage that it took. After all, he was the son of an idol maker and he had a vested interest in seeing things his father's way and his society's way; and what's more he was expected to inherit the family business.

But, while everybody else saw and worshiped multiplicity, Abraham looked at reality with eyes of wonder and concluded that there was one, invisible, incorporeal source that created, sustained, and embraced everything. Abraham was a spiritual genius. He came up with the first unified field theory and called it "Hashem."

To see Hashem, you have to dislodge from your mind—just like Abraham—society's idea of "God."

I can't say this often enough, or forcefully enough: *Forget about God.* God has been monopolized by the left brain and has been preventing our right brain from seeing the freshness of the moment, from seeing what we've never seen before. We have to look at a hand, look at a tree, look at a bird, and realize, "I don't know what that is. I call it a hand, tree, bird. But now that I look at it for the first time I don't know what it is. It's simply unbelievable. All I can really say is 'Aah.' "

Adapting yourself to reality can be scary, because it requires the courage to confront what is much bigger than yourself and to be changed by it. Spiritual seeing is an act of surrender. It takes humbleness and surrender. Most people are afraid of changing in any significant way. They say, "Oh, I'm so bored with my routine. I want a change." They want *a change,* but they don't want *to change.*

When you see reality with the eyes of wonder, you are changed every day. Life is an adventure and it's called growing.

Change and growth are what the Kabbalah is all about. It gives us a new frame of reference, so that more and more in our lives we can see reality, which is essentially seeing Hashem in our lives. They offer us a framework called the *sefirot,* which are designed to empower us to restructure our consciousness in the broadest, freest way. The Hebrew word *sefirot* is loosely translated in English as "characteristics" because it is intended to describe the various characteristics or manifestations of Hashem that we are able to perceive in the world.

So let's take a look and see.

SEEING EXERCISES

1. Open your eyes as wide as possible. Now roll them around in random directions for about ten seconds. Now try to look at the whole room at once.
2. On your way to wherever you go today try to see something you never noticed before, such as a tree, a flower, or the architectural feature of a building you pass by.
3. Practice expanding your vision. Look straight ahead while trying to catch what is happening from the corner of your eyes. Appreciate the miracle of seeing at all.
4. Pick any item—your fingers, the button on your shirt, an ant crawling on the ground—and look at it with totally fresh eyes.
5. To try drawing from the right side of the brain, find a picture you like, turn it upside down, and try copying it.
6. Can you remember seeing your teacher or boss in an unexpected place? Close your eyes and imagine the moment of surprise.

three

DIVINE COLORS OF REALITY

Once I was at the home of a great Kabbalistic master who lives in the Old City of Jerusalem. Some young people who were studying at the local college were invited to drop by and I'll never forget one young woman, who was more vocal than the rest. "What courses are you taking?" the great Kabbalist asked her.

Not realizing who he was, she replied, "Kabbalah 101."

"Kabbalah 101." he repeated. "And what in particular are you studying?"

"Well, for this weekend," she answered, "we are supposed to read the *Sefer Yetzira*.

Now, the *Sefer Yetzira,* or the *Book of Formation,* is a deep Kabbalistic work that takes many years of study to even begin to fathom. So he didn't understand what she was talking about.

"For this weekend?" he asked, perplexed.

"We have a class in it on Sunday," she explained.

"Aah," he murmured in astonishment. What was the world coming to—the *Sefer Yetzira* over the weekend made no sense to him at all.

With this memory in the forefront of my mind causing me some trepidation, I want to introduce you to the building blocks of the Kabbalistic system of reality, the *sefirot.* The *sefirot* represent an enormously complex mystical idea, but its basic understanding is an indispensable tool for seeing Hashem.

There are many books about the Kabbalah and they will often show you a diagram of the *sefirot* that looks like some kind of spiritual plumbing. Unfortunately, it is rather like showing you a picture of Versailles, one of the most exquisite buildings in the world, and showing you only an architect's blueprint. That's Versailles? Technically it is, but after you've looked at it, you still haven't seen Versailles.

Imagine looking at sheet music for the first time. It looks so technical, so abstract. Would you ever believe that all these lines and squiggles actually express beauty, passion, sadness, joy? Unless you are an accomplished musician, can you hear Beethoven's Ninth when you look at the musical notations for it? You might not even know what you are looking at.

Many people who attempt studying Kabbalah today are not "accomplished musicians." Basically, they are given sheet music that they can barely read, without a clue as to how to convert it into the *experience* of music.

What I am going to try to do is help you convert the "sheet music" of Kabbalah into the experience it is intended to represent.

Describing the Indescribable

It's in and through the *sefirot* that we see Hashem. It's in and through the *sefirot* that we encounter reality. But before we further explore the *sefirot,* let's first understand what they are not and what is necessary for seeing them.

The *Sefer Yetzira* says that the *sefirot* are "without anything." They are "no thing." Not nothing. On the contrary, they are very real, but they're "no thing." They are ethereal spiritual "qualities" through which Hashem can be seen in this world. So, while we can describe them in words, the *sefirot* can't really be understood intellectually, only experientially.

People buy books on the Kabbalah hoping to understand deep mystical concepts by reading about them. But you can't just read about the Kabbalah. Sure, you can absorb a lot of information, but in order to truly understand, you must translate what you read into experience.

The Kabbalah is referred to as the "secrets of life." After so much has been written and said about it, it seems odd that it should still be called a secret. But even after you have read and studied it, the Kabbalah still remains a secret, because you can only come to know the meaning of the Kabbalah experientially, not intellectually. In other words, someone can define chocolate for you. There is a definition for chocolate in the dictionary: "fermented, roasted, shelled, and ground cacao seeds, often combined with a sweetener or flavoring agent." But, if you've never tasted chocolate, do you know what it is by reading that definition? To understand the essence of chocolate, you have to taste it.

The Kabbalah is referred to as the secret not because no one will tell you what's written there, but because its truth must be ultimately understood experientially.

So this is key to the Kabbalah—you have to experience it. You have to let it take you somewhere.

Same with the *sefirot.* Defining the various qualities of Hashem which make up the *sefirot* is rather like defining the differences between chocolate and vanilla. Impossible to describe even if you are absolutely sure you know the difference.

The most beautiful no-things in my life are unprovable, unexplainable, yet very real. Love is a not a thing. But it's extremely real. In fact, it's more real than a lot of things I know. In just the same way, the *sefirot* are not something that you can know rationally.

Believing Is Seeing

Psalm 34 reads, "Taste and see that Hashem is good." We taste and see Hashem through faith, or what in Hebrew we call *emunah. Emunah* is not blind faith; indeed it is just the opposite.

Most people consider faith a blind, irrational acceptance of unknowable, unprovable religious dogmas.

But included in the definition of *emunah* is the fact that just because you can't explain a particular spiritual concept, it doesn't automatically mean that it is not real or unknowable. Indeed, *emunah* is true knowing and seeing. *Emunah* is superrational. *Emunah* is the level of knowing that transcends the intellectual, philosophical, rational faculty. That's why I cannot explain it in words; I just know.

Emunah is a faculty of consciousness, a way of seeing that does not operate through the intellect (although it can be supported by the intellect). *Emunah* is a direct kind of seeing through the eyes of soul. It's like knowing that red is red. I can't prove it, and I shouldn't try, because it's so incredibly obvious.

I don't know how I'm able to lift my hand. That doesn't mean I don't know how to lift my hand. I could never explain it to anyone, yet I know exactly how to do it. I know the difference between the *Mona Lisa* and a *Peanuts* cartoon. How do I know? I know. And I know the difference between vintage wine and cola. Even though they tell me it's the real thing, I know it's not. I know that the vintage wine is much better, much more valuable. I can't prove it, but I don't need to. Because I know it.

That's why the Torah starts off with a self-evident story: Hashem created heaven and earth. Torah doesn't start out telling you about Hashem's existence, and giving you proofs, and then tell you that Hashem created the world. Torah starts out with the beginning of the world, without discussion, because Hashem is self-evident.

Of course, everyone knows there is Hashem. The problem is, people don't know that they know and that they are being affected by this knowledge.

Colors and Flavors

The Kabbalah teaches that there are ten sefirot—ten qualities to reality—and that each one is like a different "color" in the spectrum of Divine light. They are not real colors; in fact, you could just as easily call them flavors. And you do not see them with your eyes or taste them with your mouth but know them with your soul. Your soul sees, tastes, and knows Hashem.

Of course, these ten qualities to reality, which are considered the ten attributes of Hashem, are from our human perspective. Indeed, everything we are discussing is relative to us, because that is the only way we know how to even approach describing the ultimate, endless reality. However, from Hashem's perspective there is only oneness. These ten attributes are, of course, the *sefirot*.

The Hebrew word *sefirot* is connected to the word *safir,* which means "sapphire," which suggests illumination. The word *sefirot* is also related to the word *mispar,* which means number, which suggests order, finitude, and is connected to the word *misapair,* which means to speak. It is through the *sefirot* that the endless light shines into the finite world. It's through the *sefirot* that the incomprehensible becomes comprehensible enough that we can speak of Hashem. The Divine light shines through the *sefirot.* By means of the *sefirot,* the endless reality is expressed through the finite, the incomprehensible becomes comprehensible.

The job of a spiritual teacher is not to be a philosopher, but a gourmet cook. A gourmet cook has the ability to bring the taste out of every ordinary cabbage, every simple bean sprout. Once, I went to someone's home to raise funds for my institute. I thought we would have a ten-minute discussion. Instead, we talked for five or six hours. I hadn't eaten all day, and I was starving. Finally I decided that instead of asking for a contribution, I would just ask for something to eat. So I said, "Could I just have an apple?"

She replied, "Oh, you must be starving. I'm so sorry!"

My hostess ran to her kitchen and made me a Salad Niçoise. Now, I'm not a big salad eater, but that's what she chose to prepare for me. Well, I took one forkful, and I have to admit I had never tasted a salad like that in my life. Because this woman was able to bring out its true taste, suddenly I had a whole new appreciation for the vegetable kingdom.

Once I tasted this woman's Salad Niçoise, I could never be satisfied with lettuce and tomato alone. The job of a spiritual teacher is to reveal Hashem in this world for all to see and taste.

Do you remember ever tasting something new? I am addicted to hanging around juice bars. I usually go to one particular juice bar and always order carrot juice. One day, I was in a real conflict because many people were coming into the juice bar and ordering exotic, strange mixes. I was going to order my regular carrot juice, but when the fellow behind the counter asked what I wanted, I took a leap of faith and said, "I want a third of apple, and a third of papaya, and a third of peach." The guy looked at me and said in astonishment, "Now that's good!" He started juicing the papaya, and I was thinking, "I'm going to hate this." I tasted it, and I couldn't believe it! I had never tasted anything like it in my life! Now, I can't go back to carrot juice. I'm hooked on my exotic concoction.

There are so many tastes in this world that we haven't experienced because we keep ordering the same stuff. We've adjusted to the menu. If people want to taste and see Hashem, they've got to become maladjusted to the menu. And be open to tasting something new that is actually ancient—the timeless no-thing.

In addition to being a gourmet cook, a spiritual teacher has to be an optometrist. Most human beings are born with perfect vision, but after a certain number of years, most people commonly develop problems in seeing. So you go to the optometrist, and you sit in a special seat, and the optometrist puts lenses of various strengths in front of you, trying different ones until you can see the chart clearly. All he's trying to do is to help you to see what's there. By giving you the right lenses, the optometrist enables you to see what is. One of the lenses is the lense of wonder. When you put on the lens of wonder, suddenly you can see Hashem, Who was there all along. So my job as a spiritual teacher is to put some wonder into your way of seeing.

It should not surprise us therefore that the Kabbalah also refers to the ten *sefirot* as different-colored lenses. Through these lenses we are able to see the many colors of the one and only ultimate reality.

So let's have a look and start to see Hashem through the colored lenses—the *sefirot*.

The Qualities of Reality

Once I was giving a seminar, and I asked everyone to look around the room and point to beauty. The first interesting result was that everyone pointed to something different. One man pointed to his wife. Another man pointed to a flower. A woman named Bea pointed to a glass menorah (a Hanukkah candelabra) that was sitting on a windowsill. I asked Bea how she saw beauty in that menorah. Did she see beauty with her physical eyes? "Well," she answered, "the glass is translucent and its delicacy has an ethereal quality. The shape is pleasing to the eye, and because it is glass, you can see the blue sky through it." But that was only her intellect giving meaning to the raw data of what she was seeing. Really, her physical eyes could only see glass molded into a nine-pronged shape. It was her soul that saw beauty and knew that it was beauty.

Another man, named Herb, pointed to a ray of sunlight shining on the white stone floor. "You think that's beauty?" I asked Herb. "That's just photons bouncing off minerals. What made you see beauty?"

Beauty is a Divine quality, one of the *sefirot.* We see it with the eyes of the soul. Beauty is one of the ten Divine colored lenses through which we can see Hashem. The incomprehensible is manifest in the comprehensible experience of beauty. The endless light shines through the quality of beauty expressed in that finite light ray bouncing off that finite stone floor.

Then I asked the seminar participants to point to the quality of power. Jackie pointed to a painting hanging in the room. We all acknowledged that it was a powerful picture. But how did we know that? It was just canvas with lines and forms painted on it. The eyes of the soul see power. Sometimes we meet a powerful person. We know this person is powerful because our soul perceives the manifestation of intrinsic power, another one of the *sefirot,* even if the person is just sitting drinking a cup of tea.

Once I was having lunch with Kirk Douglas, who at the time had grown a beard for a movie and was not so easily identifiable by his trademark dimpled chin. Yet, heads turned when he walked through the room. The other diners might not have known who he was but they knew he was somebody famous.

If you want to have an instant glimpse of how easy it is to identify the *sefirot,* take a minute to close your eyes, and try to picture life. What do you see? A baby? A field of flowers? A forest full of birds and animals? Whatever it is you are envisioning, you know it is life. You know it not with your analytical brain, but with your soul. Your soul has the capacity to see the Divine quality called life.

Now close your eyes and picture love. What do you see? Perhaps you picture a mother kissing her baby. Again, what part of you recognizes that as love? Your physical eyes see only a big creature pressing moist lips on the cheek of a little creature. But your soul knows that that is love.

When you see life, beauty, power, love, you are seeing Hashem. This is because Hashem is life, although we can't say that life is Hashem, because Hashem is not just life. He is also beauty, power, truth, wisdom, kindness, justice, and all the other *sefirot.* And even if you added them all together, you could not say that Hashem is the sum total of these qualities, because Hashem is so much more—above and beyond all this.

Now we have a better sense, through the eyes of experience, of what the *sefirot* really are—qualities of reality.

Reality, the endless light of Hashem, shines through the qualities of love and life and beauty and kindness and power and truth. These qualities are no-thing. That's why they are eternally real. All *things* pass away, but these qualities are timeless. Kabbalah teaches that what really attracts us, what really confers value, is precisely this no-thing quality.

Once an artist friend asked me to bring a very valuable painting to the United States. I asked him how much I should declare it for when I got to customs. The artist replied that the picture had cost him only fifty dollars—the price of the canvas and paints. But in fact, the picture was worth a fortune, because a connoisseur could see Hashem's beauty pouring through this piece of canvas smeared with acrylic paints. The only thing about a painting that gives it its value and attracts us is the quality of Hashem that is manifesting through it. My soul is attracted to Hashem's beauty in the painting. The artist didn't create beauty; beauty already existed; but he created a vessel for its expression. The artist knows the right combination of lines, colors and contrasts that allows Hashem's beauty to flow into this world. That's why it has value.

The Divine Attraction

What is it about a person that truly is attractive? Kabbalah says that it's the quality of Hashem. A beautiful man or woman is a channel of Hashem's beauty in the world, just as a kind man or woman is a channel for Hashem's kindness in the world.

Every human being is a unique vehicle of various Divine qualities. We are attracted to the special quality of Hashem in the person that we love. That's really what's going on. Therefore Kabbalah claims that all love is essentially directed only to Hashem.

When I'm standing in front of the Grand Canyon, am I in awe of that big pit in the ground, or am I encountering the grandeur of Hashem through the Grand Canyon? Am I in awe of the stormy sea, water surging up and down, or is it the quality of power that is manifested through the sea? The Kabbalah teaches that all awe is really only directed to Hashem.

Particularly with human beings, we become confused about the real source of the qualities we love and admire. I hear an eloquent, brilliant speaker, and I am in awe of her wisdom, but her wisdom is really not hers at all; it's actually a ray of Hashem's endless wisdom.

When I see an athlete accomplish an incredible feat, I am in awe of his strength. But that strength is really a manifestation of Hashem's power. That's why it says in the Book of Jeremiah: "Let not the wise man take pride in his wisdom. Let not the rich man brag of his riches. Let not the strong man brag of his strength. Only the one who knows me." That's the greatest accomplishment I can achieve in this world—to know Hashem as Hashem is seen in everything. Otherwise, we are looking *at* the window, rather than *through* the window.

This confusion, between what we think we love and its true Divine essence and source, is what idolatry is all about. When you read the Torah, you see that the sternest condemnations are reserved for the sin of idolatry. You think, What's the big deal about idolatry? Those primitive people liked to bow down to trees and stones, but when humanity evolved, they left behind that nonsense.

But the truth is, those idolaters were on a much higher level of sensitivity to Hashem than you and I are. They were so acutely aware of the Divine qualities shining through the phenomena of nature that they felt compelled to worship that tree and that rock as a manifestation of Hashem. Of course, the confusion, which the Torah warns us against, is to mix up Hashem with His manifestations. The sun really does express the power of Hashem. So worship Hashem, don't worship the sun!

We sophisticated, modern people make the exact same mistake.

We are attracted to something—the opposite sex, art, jewelry—and we could spend our lives chasing these things. But we suffer from confusion. It's really Hashem we want. We confuse Hashem with His manifestations. We confuse the presence with the packaging.

Sexuality is a cosmic drive. According to Torah, it's not something to be renounced. When a person has a sexual desire to unite with another person, it's not an urge for a body, it's a spark of the Divine yearning to unite with another spark of the Divine, an urge to become a channel to manifest Divine oneness. Precisely because sexual energy has such a powerful potential, it can be dangerous when it gets out of control, when it is misdirected. It's easy to forget that sexuality is meant to be directed to the service of Hashem, to life, to revealing the connection to the All and the Ultimate.

Albert, for example, is attracted to Gigi, and he's blown away by how gorgeous she looks. But when he gets to know her, he loses interest. Why? At first glance Albert is attracted to the Divine beauty of which Gigi is a manifestation. But as they start to interact, Albert may realize that Gigi is missing other Divine qualities. She might have beauty, but she lacks wisdom, truth, and kindness. She lacks love. So Albert loses interest because he wants a full manifestation of Hashem. Albert might then meet Henrietta, who doesn't embody beauty, and at first he is not attracted. But when he gets to know her, he becomes aware of her kindness, and then he becomes attracted. Did Henrietta invent kindness? No, she is simply a vehicle for Hashem's kindness. That's what Albert is attracted to.

Kabbalah tells us that when we open the eyes of our souls and begin to see Hashem, it intensifies our physical drives.

A story is told in the Jewish Oral Tradition of a student who hid under the bed of his rabbi with the hopes of learning the spiritual way to sexual intimacy. To his shock, he witnessed his rabbi having unusually passionate sex with his wife.

This was a revelation to him, because he had assumed, like so many people, that the religious would be prudish. But he learned that holiness fuels and fires up physical pleasures instead of diminishing them.

In truth, consciousness of Hashem intensifies the physical world.

When a person has consciousness of Hashem, apples taste different. They taste ultimate. When I acknowledge Hashem by reciting a blessing before I eat an apple or anything else for that matter, I taste something much greater than the fruit. I've turned this apple into an opportunity for tasting one of the flavors of Hashem. A new dimension of experience opens up that transcends the apple.

In the Talmud, various sages debate how to regard a man who is an ascetic and frequently fasts. One sage calls him a holy man. However, another sage disagrees vehemently, saying that such a person not only does not deserve to be called a holy man but should be called a sinner.

What's going on here? It's a question of education. If I think I love this apple too much, I love this painting too much, or I love this body too much, then I am confusing the manifestation of Hashem with the packaging, just like the idolaters did. If that happens, then fasting is appropriate to get me back on track. But denial of the physical is not meant to be a way of life; it's just a way of putting things in perspective. The better way is to never reach the state of confusion that requires such a bitter remedy. The better way is to enjoy it as a gift from Hashem and taste the Divine presence within it—that's the way it was intended to be.

The more we see Hashem in and through the Divine colors—*sefirot*—the more this world and all its physical pleasures glow with ultimate radiance.

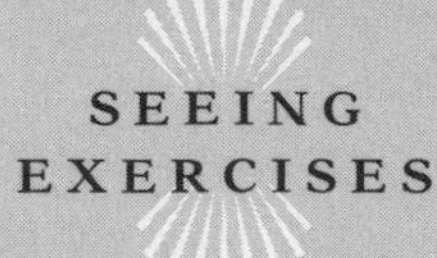

SEEING EXERCISES

1. Next time you have a meal, pay attention to the different tastes of the foods. Which are the sweetest? Which are the saltiest? How do you know that? Try to identify the ingredients.
2. The most beautiful no-things in our life are unprovable, unexplainable, and yet very real. List the five most important no-things in your life.
3. In your travels today look for things or people who express the quality of beauty, life, love, and power.
4. Next time you see a beautiful woman or a handsome man, try to define what is beautiful or handsome about him or her.
5. Can you remember meeting someone who on first impression was unattractive, but after you got to know the person proved very appealing? What about your perception changed? What is it about that person that you didn't see at first?

four

COMMUNAL CONSCIOUSNESS

"Daddy, where is Hashem?"
"Son, wherever you let Him in."

How do we open our souls' eyes to let Hashem in? To answer this question, we will now begin to explore the *sefirot,* the ten qualities of Hashem, one by one in detail.

The first of the *sefirot* that we will examine is *malhus,* which is the power to see all the other qualities. *Malhus* is an attribute of Hashem within us. This attribute is consciousness itself. In other words, as mysterious as it may sound, the consciousness within us to see Hashem actually comes from Hashem.

Malhus literally means "kingdom," that is, a collective of people who acknowledge a particular king. However, the Kabbalah intends a much broader definition—*malhus* really means that you experience yourself as a participant in a communal consciousness that recognizes and acknowledges Hashem not only as a Higher Power but as the Ultimate Supreme Sovereign Power. That collective recognition of Hashem channels the Divine Majestic Presence into this world.

The Kabbalah says, "There is no king without a nation." This point requires deep exploration. It may make sense that in the human world a king is dependent on having subjects who acknowledge his sovereignty. The last emperor of China ceased to be emperor when there were no longer people who bowed when he entered the room. Even after the Communist government had exiled him, as long as people recognized him and acknowledged him as their sovereign, he was, in a very real sense, still a king, albeit without the power to rule. But Hashem is reality, so how can Hashem be dependent on human acknowledgment?

The world that you and I live in is a product of our perception of reality. The philosopher Immanuel Kant probed this concept. He asked: Do we see reality or do we see our perception of reality? Kant's answer, of course, is that we do not see reality, but only our perception of reality. In other words, is this world reality? No, this world is your perception of reality. Therefore, the focus and clarity of your consciousness will determine the kind of world you live in.

Imagine three people sitting next to each other in a doctor's waiting room. Are they sitting in the same room? Let's say the first person walked in and complained, "Oh, how small this room is!" The second person entered, and exclaimed, "Look how bright this room is." The third person came in, and thought, Ugh, what a messy room. Now, they are sitting inches apart, but they are not in the same room. The first person is sitting in a small room, feeling really cramped. The second person is sitting in a light room, feeling cheerful. The third person is sitting in a messy room, feeling disgusted.

Essentially, what you see is what you get. The world you live in is a product of what you are looking at and are willing to see. This is expressed in the Zohar's commentary on the story of Jacob as he goes to Egypt to be reunited with his long-lost son, Joseph. Jacob has misgivings about leaving the land of Israel, even to see his beloved son. Hashem appears to Jacob and says, "Jacob, don't worry. Joseph will close your eyes." The basic text of the Kabbalah queries, what does this mean? According to Torah, when a person passes away, someone must close the person's eyes. The Zohar explains that the colors and textures and shapes of this world exist in your eyes. In order to enter a new world, a higher world, after death, the soul must first leave this world. This world exists *in one's eyes,* so the eyes must be closed in order to take leave of this world and see a higher world. Hashem is announcing to Jacob that he is going to die in Egypt and that Joseph will be there to close his eyes to this world, so that he will be able to enter, that is, see, the next world.

Is the Zohar saying that this world is an illusion? No. The Zohar is saying that this world is your subjective perception. Your consciousness of reality determines the world you're in. Your consciousness of Hashem determines how much of the light and the truth of Hashem will be allowed into your world. To the extent that you acknowledge Hashem, Hashem will be in your life. This is a very crucial idea. Although Hashem exists, Hashem is not revealed in your perceptual world unless you actively acknowledge and invite Hashem in.

Expanded Consciousness

The Talmud says that a beautiful spouse, a beautiful house, and beautiful objects expand a person's mind. Once I was visiting a friend who was in the throes of deciding whether to live in Israel or America. Moving to Israel would have meant a boost to his spiritual life, but a significant drop in his standard of living. He quoted to me this verse from the Talmud. "I think I could probably have a more beautiful house if I lived in America," he told me. "I could make more money. I could afford more beautiful furnishings. So why shouldn't I stay here in Chicago?"

I replied: "The Talmud says those things will expand your mind. You have to decide how you are going to fill your expanded mind. If you have little to fill it with, you will feel very empty."

In this age, there is a lot of talk about expanded consciousness, but much less talk about how to fill that expanse once it is achieved. I have had students in my Isralight seminars who consider themselves very spiritual. Unfortunately, they are often the ones who seem blind to the needs of others and to their own responsibilities—they don't clean up their dishes, or pitch in with chores. They think they have an expanded consciousness, but of what? If you're conscious of yourself, then you're full of yourself, and your consciousness is very narrow.

True expanded consciousness is a collective, communal consciousness of Hashem—not a self-absorbed spirituality trip. It inspires us to want to help others. We treat each other with the love and respect due to royal subjects. This kind of expanded consciousness leads to turning this world into a kingdom filled with Divine majestic presence.

To the extent that we open our eyes to Hashem and fill the vessel of our consciousness with Hashem, Hashem will fill our world. It also works the other way around. To the extent that we deny Hashem, Hashem will not be in our world.

The Zohar, the basic text of Kabbalah, says that consciousness is nothing in and of itself. Its value is only that which it receives. *Malhus* serves only as a channel for receiving the lights and the blessings of the divine qualities and for transmitting them into our world.

A friend of mine had an unpleasant experience with the mother of one of his students. The student was about to be ordained a rabbi and this greatly upset his mother, who considered organized religion to be backward and fanatical. She was very nasty and cynical about her son's religious convictions. They were on the way to the ceremony when she turned to my friend and said, "Basically, I don't believe in God."

My friend replied, "OK, fine! Don't believe in God." He was the first religious person to respond to her that way; others had always tried to convince her of God's existence.

"What?" she exclaimed in surprise.

"You don't want to believe in God?" he said. "Fine, so live in a godless world."

That's essentially the choice we have. If we don't want to believe in Hashem, then Hashem won't be in our world. That doesn't mean Hashem isn't real. Hashem is real, but not for those who choose to deny that truth.

In other words, if I've never tasted papaya, then there's no flavor of papaya in my life. Whether it's real or not for others, it's not in my life. If I'm blind to the color red, then red will not be one of the colors in my life. If mammals do not see colors, they live in a colorless world. If I'm not willing to see Hashem, then my world is godless.

Experiencing the Presence of Hashem

The Talmudic Sages taught: "Everything is in the hands of Hashem except awe of Hashem."

The Hebrew word for awe, *yera,* means both "awe" and "will see." Everything is in the hands of Hashem, except for our acknowledging and seeing and being in awe of Hashem. If we are in awe, we will see Hashem. If we are not in awe, if we are not open to seeing Hashem, then Hashem is not in our world. It's that simple and that serious.

A student of mine, Tina, was traveling in Bangkok, where she met Joe, another tourist, whom she immediately recognized as her soulmate. Tina was ecstatic. Joe, however, as much as he liked Tina was not ready to change his plans to pursue a relationship with her and was preparing to continue his travels in India. But then Joe's bag mysteriously disappeared, along with his passport, his credit cards, and his plane tickets. He was forced to cancel his plans while he unraveled the mess. Tina recognized the presence of Hashem in this turn of events and was grateful and happy, but Joe was aggravated. To him this was just a colossal pain in the neck. Needless to say, Joe and Tina ended up spending a great deal of time together wading through the intricacies of Thai bureaucracy, and by the time Joe was ready to leave again, he didn't want to at all. He had come to see Tina as the woman of his dreams. They returned home from Bangkok engaged to be married.

Some people experience constant Divine presence, which means they see and feel Hashem's care and guidance in their lives. They need $800 to pay for a car repair, and an unexpected check for $800 arrives in the mail. They miss a bus, so they get on the next bus, and the person they sit down next to turns out to be a friend from twenty years ago.

Why are such experiences not part of everyone's daily life? Because, as I said earlier, what you see is what you get.

To the extent that when we build our awareness, expand our consciousness, and acknowledge that Hashem is the power directing the show, we see how Hashem runs the show for us.

Each one of us has a choice. You can believe that this world is filled with the presence of Hashem, Who cares about it and guides it. Or you can believe that this world is one big accident, a chaotic mess. The choice is yours. But remember: What you believe creates the world you live in.

Once I was dating a woman, whom I'll call Daphne, whom I loved very much. I wanted to marry her but it took me a long time to realize that she simply could not acknowledge my love. I did everything in my power to show her that I loved her. Daphne had such a poor image of herself, however, that she couldn't believe that anyone could love her. It didn't matter how much I professed my love to her, how many bouquets of flowers I sent her. She couldn't see my love. So, in a way, it wasn't there for her.

Everyone is thirsty for love, but how much love you can receive is dependent on how much you believe someone can love you. The more you acknowledge and believe in Hashem, the more you receive and see Hashem in your life.

During the Gulf War, thirty-nine Scud missiles were launched against Israel. Miraculously, only one person died as a direct result of all those missiles. It was unbelievable. We sat in our sealed rooms, wearing our gas masks and listening to the radio. We heard that Scuds were flying toward Israel. They never announced where they fell, but everyone knew that most of them fell near Ramat Gan, a very densely populated city next to Tel Aviv. Then, awhile later, we heard, "No casualties." During the war, I remember hearing an interview with the past minister of defense. After yet another attack with no casualties, the interviewer asked him. "What do you have to say about this?" He answered hesitatingly, "I would have to say this is a miracle." I could hear the incredible resistance in his voice; he was trying very hard not to admit the possibility that miracles could happen. The truth is, if you don't want to believe in miracles, you won't see miracles in your life.

Building Blocks of Consciousness

How would I act if I really believed that Hashem's presence filled my life, my home, my office, my city, my world? How would I speak to my wife and kids? How would I treat the stranger? To the extent that I think, speak, and act in accordance with this heightened awareness, to that extent, Hashem can be present in my world. It's not just a matter of believing and saying so. We have to acknowledge Hashem's presence in the world constantly, by how we conduct our relationships, how we speak to others, how we eat our lunch, how we do virtually everything. Spirituality without a daily discipline is just a hobby.

Once I was asked to officiate at the bar mitzvah of a boy who lived in an ashram. This particular ashram, which was located in India, was comprised mostly of Jews. The guru told the boy's mother to take her son to the Western Wall in Jerusalem and celebrate his bar mitzvah there. So, many of the Jewish people from this ashram came to Jerusalem. They looked for an open-minded rabbi willing to officiate at this unusual bar mitzvah, and they came to me. Sure, why not? I thought.

After the ceremony, we went back to someone's home for a celebration. There the boy gave a bar mitzvah speech like I'd never heard before. He said: "I want to thank the One and the Only, All in One and One in All." This thirteen-year-old boy really impressed me with his lofty, mystical articulations. He and his fellow ashram dwellers were very spiritual people.

After the speech, everyone was invited to have some food—all strictly vegetarian. Everyone was barefoot, having left their shoes at the door. The meal was a buffet, so after the guests got their food, they sat down cross-legged on the floor and ate.

I had three of my kids with me and we helped ourselves and sat down on the floor like everyone else. At that point, my son Nuri, then five years old, looked at me and exclaimed, appalled, "Daddy, you won't believe it. They didn't say a blessing before they ate."

His shock was acute, and he may have missed it, but the irony struck me as sad. I have met self-acclaimed, highly spiritual people, who have the consciousness to be vegetarians, and the humility to take off their shoes and even sit on the floor. But when it comes to consuming their food, they just stuff themselves. They do not even pause and meditate for a moment, to appreciate the food as a Divine gift. On the other hand, my kids, who I can guarantee are spiritually unsophisticated, would never think of popping a crumb into their mouths without first acknowledging Hashem as the source of the food.

For a thirteen-year-old to talk about "the One in the All and the All in the One" is impressive. But how does one take this high level of philosophical content and turn it into an everyday consciousness. How do we bring it into the office, bring it into the kitchen, bring it into the living room, bring it into the bedroom?

It is not only through a collection of very deep ideas that I build consciousness of Hashem. I need a daily concrete way to walk the talk. The so-called good deeds and rituals of the Torah's spiritual tradition are designed to be building blocks for nurturing and concretizing consciousness all day long, so that I can channel Hashem's presence into the world and into my life.

By increasing my consciousness of Hashem, I thereby allow the light of Hashem and all the gifts of spiritual wealth to pour into the world. Few realize the true goodness in deeds and the real richness in rituals. These deeds and rituals are really invitations to Hashem. What we are saying in both words and actions is, "Hashem, I want to get You into my life!"

When I reach into my pocket and give charity to the beggar on the street, when I smile at the person next to me in the supermarket line, when I extend myself to help my neighbor unload heavy packages, when I spend quality time with my kids by reading with them, I am inviting Hashem into my world. All these good deeds actually become invitations to bring the Divine into our world.

Exiling Hashem

I have choice. I can nourish the consciousness of Hashem through my speech, thoughts, and actions. Or I can neglect it; I could choose to filter out the divine qualities from my awareness and thus live in a godless world. Kabbalah refers to that state as "the exile of Hashem's presence." In other words, I can throw Hashem out of the world.

An amazing verse in Psalm 119 says, "I am a stranger on earth." According to some commentaries, the "I" refers to Hashem, who considers Himself present in this world, but unrecognizable by anyone.

In another astounding verse from Isaiah 43:12, we are told, "You are My witnesses. I am Hashem." The Midrash comments, "If you are My witnesses, I am Hashem. But if you are not My witnesses, I am not Hashem." What does that mean? It's an unbelievable idea. Hashem depends on our acknowledgment in word and deed in order to enter into our world. For Hashem to appear in our world we must be Hashem's witness. Hashem depends, so to speak, on our consciousness in order to enter into our world.

I once had a student who though raised in a religious home didn't believe in God. He himself didn't understand why he didn't believe in God. He attended religious schools, learned to say prayers and blessings, and was taught that there is a God. His parents, however, although they professed belief in God, treated people like dirt. In other words, their behavior denied God. Their denigration of other people demonstrated their total lack of a consciousness of Hashem's presence in this world. Although in words they said, "We believe in God," in action they said they really didn't. And actions speak louder than words. Thus, they raised their son in a godless world. Naturally, he concluded that there is no God, because that was true for the home he grew up in—Hashem was not present there.

Of course, Hashem does not need our acknowledgment in order to exist, but Hashem does need our acknowledgment in order to exist in our homes, in our workplaces, in our schools, in our perceptual world.

Without our consciousness, the light of Hashem cannot illuminate our world, so we find ourselves in a frightening darkness, and the darkness that results from the absence of Hashem's light creates the space for evil.

I am always amazed when I take off in an airplane on a dark and gloomy cloudy day at how bright it actually is once we get past the clouds. I always try to remind myself during dark times in my life that the light is actually still shining. I just need to pierce the clouds and let the sunshine in. The darkness comes only because something is blocking the light.

We can block Hashem's light from the world by creating cloudy consciousness through our thoughts, speech, and actions. If we close our eyes to seeing Hashem, we'll create a dark world that is seemingly governed by chaotic, meaningless forces that promote destructive behavior.

Good and True

According to the Kabbalah, the first man and woman caused the Divine Presence to withdraw from this world. When they ate from the Tree of Knowledge of Good and Bad, they blocked the light of Hashem. What was their mistake? They assumed that they could create their own reality and determine for themselves what truly is.

You can't create your own reality or truth. But you can create your own perceptual world that blocks out the light of reality. The snake was really saying to Adam and Eve, "If you eat from the Tree of Knowledge of Good and Bad, you too will be creators of worlds." And that's true. You can create your own world through the knowledge of good and bad. You can decide what is bad and decide what is good for yourself, but it might not be true. It might not represent what's real, what actually is. You can live in your own imaginative world but it might not reflect what's really going on. You can choose to live in a world of lies and put yourself out of touch with reality.

This is what the Kabbalah is talking about when it says that Adam and Eve separated the Tree of Knowledge from the Tree of Life. We tend to forget that there were two trees in the garden. The Tree of Life represented reality as it is. The Tree of Knowledge represented our perception and consciousness of reality. However, our understanding of reality doesn't create reality. It simply creates our image of reality, our perceptual world. The challenge of Adam and Eve, which we have inherited, is to see reality the way it is. To the extent that we clearly see reality, Hashem's truth can fill our world.

The Kabbalah explains that Adam and Eve were supposed to eat of the Tree of Knowledge and the Tree of Life together, thereby unifying their perception with reality. Their perception of what is had to be one with what truly is. So that what they understood to be good was also true.

After their error, all human beings suffered from the illusion that perception in and of itself was reality, rather than only a vehicle for receiving reality. By separating consciousness from reality, the first man and woman created the possibility of a godless world. We began living in our imaginative world, disconnected from reality and deluding ourselves that it is real. We have been able to feel good about doing something or eating something that in truth is deadly. We could convince ourselves that if it feels good, it must be all right, real, and true, and that if it feels bad, it couldn't be real and right—it must be wrong.

The Cornerstone

According to the Kabbalah, Abraham was an antidote to the error of Adam and Eve. He began repairing the broken vessel of consciousness and bridging the gap between perception and reality. And thereby he initiated the return of the presence of Hashem into our world.

Abraham is important not just because he was a saintly individual, but because he brought Hashem back into this world. He set the cornerstone for a new world consciousness. Abraham was the first person to acknowledge an ultimate, transcendent, all-inclusive reality. In other words, he was the first to see it like it is and invite Hashem back into the world.

In contrast, the pagan world around him worshiped the disparate forces of nature and created a perceptual world of separate, conflicting powers, personifying gods at war with each other. Because that's the way they saw reality, that's the world they lived in—their perception influenced their behavior accordingly.

To be in sync with a chaotic world of warring powers, one necessarily creates a society where everyone is ultimately separate from everyone else, where every fiefdom is perpetually fighting every other fiefdom, and where one person's gain means his neighbor's loss, a wild, chaotic life devoid of ultimate meaning.

The pagan world was devoid of Hashem, devoid of an ultimate, unifying reality that made human beings accountable for their actions. The world they saw and the world they created through their behavior and relationships was totally different from Abraham's world.

In the pagan world, the rules were:

- anything goes
- might makes right
- the survival of the fittest is all that matters
- if I can get away with it, it's okay
- anything is fair in love and war

To the people around him, Abraham was a guy from another planet. That's why they called him an *ivri,* from which the word "Hebrew" derives. *Ivri* means "someone from the other side."

Abraham was weird; he behaved strangely. He went out of his way to help other people, including strangers. He was compassionate, kind, concerned for the fate of even the wicked citizens of Sodom and Gomorrah. According to pagan values, he was crazy. In a fragmented world of conflicting forces, what would motivate someone to be unselfish?

Abraham lived in a different world because he acknowledged reality as the one and indivisible living Hashem, who loves and embraces all. Abraham's love and care for his fellow human beings flowed naturally from his worldview. Thus he brought Hashem into the world through his thought, word, and deed.

The new world that Abraham created by his consciousness reflected Hashem's truth. Since Abraham was attuned to what is (actually, *Who* is), he was open to hearing the word of Hashem, and indeed he did. Hashem said to Abraham, "I will make you into a great nation. I will bless you and make your name great. You will become a blessing."

How can a person "become a blessing"? The Midrash explains that Hashem said to Abraham, "Until now the power of blessing was in My hands. Now I'm giving the power of blessing to you."

Taking the power of blessing into our own hands is like having control over the light. The Kabbalah says that you and I have the dimmer switch in our hands. We can either turn the light of Hashem up, creating a whole new, brilliant, radiant world imbued with the presence of Hashem, or we can turn the dimmer down, creating a dark, gloomy, ugly, godless world. Our consciousness, which is nurtured by our thoughts, speech, and actions, becomes the vessel to receive the divine qualities and the vehicle to transmit those qualities into our perceptual world. Abraham was the master of blessing, but every one of us can "become a blessing."

The Midrash relates a strange parable. A king is lost in a dark alley at night. He is groping and stumbling around in this alley. Suddenly a friend looks out of his window and sees the king, lost in the alley. He lights a torch so that the king can see where he is going. The Midrash says that the friend was Abraham. Hashem said to Abraham: "Go before Me," meaning, light the path for Me. That's what Abraham did. He, so to speak, enabled Hashem to enter the world by "turning on a light," that is, by awakening a whole new awareness, a new consciousness. That new consciousness was *malhus*.

The idolaters believed in many powers and forces, but not in one supreme, all-embracing reality to whom all are accountable. Abraham came up with the first unified field theory. He insisted that reality was not merely a random host of fragmented forces. Abraham saw design, purpose, community. He saw a kingdom. He proclaimed publicly, wherever he went, "I'm part of the kingdom; you're part of the kingdom; we must be responsible for each other; we must love and care for one another." And that consciousness of kingdom opened the way for Hashem's majestic entrance back into the world.

The New World

Fundamental to Abraham's community consciousness was a sense of the interdependence of all the parts within the whole. Hashem went on to tell Abraham, "Through you *all the families of the earth* will be blessed."

No person is an island. Your awareness influences my awareness; my awareness influences your awareness. Not only can we be a blessing or a curse to each other, but we inevitably *are* a blessing or a curse to each other and all those around us. If I am blocking the light of Hashem out of my world, then I am also casting a shadow on my neighbor's world.

Imagine that we are all in a boat together. Then one fellow, who feels thirsty, decides to drill a hole under his seat so he can have a drink. Of course, we all start screaming: "What are you doing, we are all going to drown!"

"Mind your own business!" he snaps back. "This hole is under my seat, it's a free world and I can do as I please."

This is the absurd attitude and behavior of people who are missing communal consciousness, excluding themselves from being part of the collective acknowledgment of Hashem. It's important to understand that we must be concerned not only with promotion of the awareness of Hashem, but also promotion of a communal awareness of Hashem. Many of the guidelines and directives of the Torah's spiritual tradition are for the sake of creating and strengthening community.

Once, my father and I were on the beach. We saw a man with his two sons. After they had finished their picnic, the man took the garbage, and threw it into the ocean. My father was appalled. He walked over to the man and said, "What are you doing?"

The man replied, "What's it your business?"

"What do you mean, 'What's it my business?' " my father persisted. "It's our business! What are you doing?"

The man retorted, "I'm throwing the garbage out."

"How can you throw your garbage into the sea?" my father demanded.

"What's it your business?" the man sneered.

That man had no community consciousness, no *malhus*. Community consciousness is the vessel that receives the light of Hashem. That man made it impossible for Hashem's presence to enter the world, to enter the sea that day, to enter the beach. He drove Hashem from the world.

A friend of mine was once at a rock concert at a stadium near Tel Aviv. The arena was packed, despite the high price of the tickets. As my friend was making his way toward his seat, he noticed a family climbing over the fence. They looked to the left and to the right to make sure that nobody was watching, and then they started lifting the kids over the fence. My friend went over to them and asked, "What are you doing?"

The father of the family answered, "It's not your business."

My friend looked him in the eye and said, "You looked left, you looked right, but you forgot to look up."

This man actually thought that nobody, including Hashem,

would see him. He lived in a world devoid of such awareness. Hashem was not in his world. And he was giving his kids their real education on that fence. He was teaching them that Hashem doesn't see. And even though Hashem does see, his kids would never see that Hashem sees. Therefore Hashem would not be in their world.

Unfortunately, these examples are not isolated instances. A sense of community is greatly lacking in most parts of the modern world. Self-sufficiency, individuality, and independence are valued more than interdependence and community. This was driven home to me during one recent visit to the United States. I was staying with a family in a very wealthy area. I went for a walk alone on a Sunday morning. I couldn't have been more than two blocks from my hosts' house, but I got lost. I didn't know how to get back to where they lived. So I thought, OK, I'll ask somebody on the street for directions. Then I realized that there was nobody on the street. In my neighborhood in Jerusalem, I have to allow double the amount of time to walk anywhere because of the number of people I "meet and greet" on the way. But here, nobody was walking on the sidewalks.

So I thought, OK, I'll knock on someone's door. Then I became acutely aware that one can't knock on someone's door, because every estate has a sign outside warning, ARMED RESPONSE, BEWARE OF DOG, or NEVER MIND THE DOG, BEWARE OF OWNER. I realized that everybody here lived in his or her own world. So how was I going to get somebody to tell me how to get back?

Finally, I peered through a hedge and saw a man sitting on his lawn. I said, "Excuse me." The guy jumped. I rushed to reassure him. "I'm harmless." I said, "I just want to know how do I get to so-and-so's house."

"Never heard of him!"

"OK, well, do you know where such-and-such a street is?"

"No, never heard of the street either."

I said, "I'm sure this street is only about two blocks away. Are you sure you've never heard of it? How long have you been living here?"

"Fifteen years!"

I thought that was strange. Later, I shared this story with a fellow I know who lives in California. He said, "That's not strange. I live in a neighborhood where the homes are built on cliffs, closely packed together. I don't know the names of my neighbors, and I'm sure they don't know my name, and I've been living there for ten years.

There's no sense of community. Everybody lives in his or her own world. But if you really want to let in the light of the all-embracing, ultimate reality, then you have to plug into a collective consciousness. Through that collective consciousness, more of the light of Hashem will come into your life and the lives of others. Then, more of the blessings of beauty and truth and providence and wisdom can flow into our world.

Community doesn't mean we are all the same. A true community is like a corporation: Everyone has a different responsibility and plays a different role, yet each contributes to the whole. Indeed, the different roles are essential to the corporation's success. While the CEO may be a marketing genius, he can do nothing without the person in product development who is the creative genius, and they both depend on the detail-conscious guy in the mail room who makes sure things go where they should. If the company consisted of nothing but marketing geniuses, it wouldn't succeed—what would it sell? If it had only creative geniuses, it wouldn't succeed because the world would remain uninformed of its products. And it wouldn't matter how organized and brilliant the top management was, if the people on the bottom didn't do their jobs well.

When people have collective consciousness, they appreciate such differences and understand each other's individual importance. In a community, uniformity depends on shared ideals and values within a structure that all respect. In a community, in a corporation, in any organizational structure, there is a commitment to unity, structure, teamwork, the mission statement, and team rules. Most of all, there is a sense of the common good, of working together for mutual benefit, and of needing one another to achieve collective, as well as individual, goals.

In the final analysis *malhus* gets down to this: Without a commitment to each other, there is no community. Without a community, there is no community consciousness, and without a community consciousness, there can be no consciousness of Hashem. We won't see Hashem in our world.

SEEING EXERCISES

1. Can you recall being with someone who saw the place you were in very differently from you? What was the difference?
2. Can you remember a situation in which you were sure the way you saw it was the only way, but then realized that you had a narrow slice of the picture and were therefore wrong?
3. Define your relationship to community. Some of the questions you might consider: Are you part of a community? What are the beliefs and shared values that unite the community? What could you do to better unify your community? Is your community elevating your appreciation for life? If yes, how so? If not, why not? How does your community acknowledge Hashem?
4. Consider writing a mission statement for your community? How do you see your role in fulfilling that mission?
5. Can you think of any values or divine qualities that are now present in your life that were nonexistent for you years ago? What change in your attitude do you recall that might have opened you to seeing these qualities? What do you do on a daily basis to acknowledge and channel these qualities into your world?

6. Can you recall Providence intervening in your life? What was the most amazing instance of such intervention?
7. Can you see a repeating pattern of events happening to you in your life?
8. Did you ever love someone who could not see your love? What do you think was blocking his or her vision?
9. If you really felt Hashem's presence today how would you act differently toward your friends, spouse, boss, parents, children, and so on?
10. Do you have daily routines or rituals through which you invite Hashem into your life? Can you think of one new thing that you can do today to invite Hashem into your life?

five

LETTING THE BLESSINGS FLOW

The second of the ten *sefirot* is life—more accurately, the synergy of life, its spiritual wealth and wholeness. In Hebrew it is called *yesod,* which means "foundation" or "basis."

This power of life synergy is the "basis" of everything we are talking about. According to the Kabbalah, the entire theme of life is Hashem's desire to be present and manifest in our world. *Yesod* reveals the awesome secret of how Hashem contracts His infinite spiritual qualities in order to enter into our finite consciousness. People think that in order to see and meet Hashem, they will have to leave or nullify this finite world; they think they must transcend time and space. But this is not true. The power of *yesod* pulls together and synthesizes all the other *sefirot* whereby Hashem meets us in our world. And now all we have to do is open the door of consciousness—open the eyes of soul.

To fully understand *yesod,* we will have to wait until we examine the other eight *sefirot*—will, wisdom, understanding, kindness, justice, truth, beauty, power—because this one quality is the synergy of them all.

The other *sefirot* are like the many colors of an artist's palette. *Yesod* is like the finished painting. Consider the difference between an artist's palette and her painting. The very same colors appear in both places, but who would want to hang a palette full of individual blobs of paint on the wall? In the painting, the colors come together and the end result becomes greater than the sum of its parts. The life force channeled by this painting comes through the synergy of the colors uniting together within it.

Yesod is life, zest, vitality, goodness, wholeness, abundance, and blessing. And we know it when we see it. We can see life or the absence of it. We see people all around us who are just not alive. They're breathing, they're walking, but they're not embodying the full spirit of life. They don't have zest or vitality, the power of *yesod.* They are not acting, speaking, or thinking in a way that nurtures the community's consciousness of life so they can become a vehicle for it in the world.

Similarly, we can see goodness, which a human being achieves by fulfilling his or her intended purpose. When the Torah relates the story of creation, it ends the recitation of the events of each day with: "And Hashem saw that it was good." What did Hashem see about each creation that made it good? Hashem saw that it was complete—it fulfilled its intended purpose. But, after the creation of Adam, the Torah keeps mum. This is because the first human being had yet to actualize his potential. He had not yet fulfilled his intended purpose. He was not yet whole and complete. And why were the other elements complete at creation, while the human being was not? Human beings, unlike the rest of creation, have free will. Only after we make the right choices do we fulfill our purpose, achieve wholeness, and embody divine goodness.

Again, we know it when we see it.

And we can also see abundance and blessing, just as we can see their absence.

I once came across a billboard that said, MANY POOR SOULS LIVE IN MILLION DOLLAR HOUSES. From personal experience I know this is true. I've walked into the mansions of multimillionaires, and in certain such places, I have felt a lack of spiritual wealth and blessing. These places were filled with expensive furniture and rugs and a million dollars worth of art, but the emptiness was palpable. Although each house was an outstanding and elegant piece of architecture and interior design, it wasn't a home. It missed its purpose. It was without blessing. It lacked *yesod.* Although people lived there, it was lifeless.

Feeling Connected

Through the colored lens of *yesod,* I am able to see Hashem as the whole living reality, the nurturing source of all blessing and goodness.

Yesod completes *malhus.* Life completes consciousness. Consciousness, in and of itself, is nothing. It is merely a vessel; what gives it value is the content. Life, the synergy of all the Divine qualities, is that content.

The Torah quotes the Patriarch Jacob as saying "I have everything." Jacob is referring, of course, to his relationship with Hashem. Thus we learn that when we have a consciousness of Hashem, the ultimate living reality and source of all blessing and goodness, then we really do have it all. What more could we ask for?

We need to unite *yesod* and *malhus* so as to combine life, vitality, and abundance with consciousness, order, and structure. It's all about embodying life in thought, speech, and action within a community context and thereby putting life in order.

What happens if you don't unify the two? Then you have consciousness without divine content, which is rather like having a wire without electricity. There is no spark, no connection, no energy.

A self-serving community has no purpose beyond itself. It is a corporation without a mission statement. It is an organization without a cause. It is a computer without a program. It is useless.

Imagine a person who meditates all day and does nothing to actively change and improve this world. Such meditation is only self-absorption and lacks the blessing acquired only through service. Consciousness in and of itself is nothing. Consciousness without divine content is a body without a soul. It is death.

Of course, you can also have the opposite situation. You can have electricity without a wire, or a soul without a body. Electricity needs wires to flow through in order for it to be productive. The soul needs a body in order to accomplish its purpose in this world. You can't access life or channel blessing without participating in a community consciousness that has law, order, and higher purpose.

Successful productive living requires both the wires and the electricity that flows through them: *malhus and yesod.* So, what happens when you connect *yesod* and *malhus?* You experience feeling connected and "plugged in."

And then you know what it means to feel disconnected. Sometimes there's order in your life, but for what? You feel a lack of aliveness to get you moving. You've got the car but no gas. Or sometimes, you feel full of zest, but your life is a mess, without order or direction, so the energy dissipates without accomplishing anything. It's as if someone hung a big sign on your life: OUT OF ORDER!

When life functions at its optimum, when life flows into consciousness, *yesod* into *malhus,* we have a state that is embodied by a *tzaddik,* a person who is the epitome of goodness, who is holy.

Who is a *tzaddik?* When I was growing up, there was a picture in our living room of several old sages with pale faces, long white beards, and thick glasses, studying Torah around a table piled high with thick tomes. The room looked gloomy and dark and they presented a sad sight, all hunched over from years of sitting there, never getting any exercise.

That was my concept of a *tzaddik,* a person who has attained the ultimate goals of life. And I sure didn't want to end up being one of them. Therefore, I was shocked to learn that the Torah's prototype of the *tzaddik* was none other than Joseph, the youthful, dynamic, charismatic lad who became the viceroy of Egypt. The oral tradition says that Joseph was so handsome that the girls would climb the walls to try and get a look at him. When he was sold into slavery, his master's wife, the sexy Mrs. Potiphar, was irresistibly attracted to him. In Egypt he became a symbol for fertility. That's really what a *tzaddik* is—a live wire. And that live wire transmits zest for life, goodness, and blessing. When you are in the presence of a *tzaddik,* you sense that flow of energy and you feel high just being in the same room.

I remember once meeting Rabbi Raphael Levin, the son of Rabbi Aryeh Levine, whose life was portrayed in a wonderful book called *A Tzaddik in Our Times.* Rabbi Raphael is, like his father, considered a true *tzaddik.* He shook my hand, taking his time about it, not letting go right away, and suddenly I felt like I was becoming spiritually charged. The feeling didn't leave me for the whole day.

A *tzaddik* charges everyone around him. A *tzaddik* brings energy into order. In fact, he is more than a live wire; he is like the switch that completes the circuit so that the electricity flows. That's why we are told that even when a *tzaddik* passes away, he or she is still alive.

The opposite of a *tzaddik* is a *rasha,* or an evil person, who is dead even when he is alive. An evil person disconnects *yesod* from *malhus.* He becomes a circuit breaker. Life flows into the circuit of consciousness, but a *rasha* breaks the circuit. He causes a separation between community and life.

How? First of all, an evil person doesn't even acknowledge that he is living in a community. He proclaims: "I'm self-defined, self-sufficient, independent, and I don't belong to any higher order. I don't have to abide by anybody's rules. I am my own man. I am my own boss." A *rasha* doesn't acknowledge Hashem, therefore Hashem is not in his life. And he cannot be a channel for Hashem. Instead of feeling charged when you are with this person, you feel drained, as if all of your energy is being sucked out of you.

Shortcut to Blessings

Those of us who have yet to reach the level of a *tzaddik* may be wondering if there is some shortcut to the spiritual wealth of life. One of the most powerful and immediate ways to connect the circuit, switch on life, and let the blessings flow is *tzedaka,* that is, charity. It is no coincidence that this word sounds similar to *tzaddik,* as both are derived from the same Hebrew root.

The Talmud teaches: "*Tzedaka* saves from death." When we need an incredible influx of life force—because we are facing impending physical death or impending spiritual death—the act of giving to charity can be one of the most powerful antidotes.

As proof for the statement, the Talmud tells the incredible story of the daughter of the famous Rabbi Akiva, who lived some two thousand years ago. A stargazer told Rabbi Akiva that his daughter would die on the day of her wedding. Rabbi Akiva replied that just because it is written in the stars, it does not mean it has to happen, because we can make choices that overturn our destinies.

As it turned out, however, on the day of her wedding, the young bride was getting ready when, unbeknownst to her, a poisonous snake slithered into the room and crawled up the back of her dress. Unaware, she continued to put on her wedding bonnet. In those days, brides wore elaborate headdresses affixed with large hat pins. The snake was ready to bite her just as she inserted a pin and pierced one of the eyes of the snake. Then she put in the other pin and it pierced the other eye and killed the snake.

Still unaware of what had happened, she went out to greet her father, who was shocked to see a dead snake dangling from her hair. Realizing the narrowness of her escape, he asked, "What did you do that you succeeded in saving yourself from death?"

She thought for a moment, then remembered that earlier in the day as everyone in the house was busy preparing for the wedding, she heard a knock at the door. All the others were too preoccupied with their duties, but she, the bride, in the midst of beautifying herself, heard the knock and took the time to answer. Standing there was a person asking for money, so she gave him a few coins.

Rabbi Akiva nodded knowingly, "*Tzedaka* saves a person from death."

Why should giving a few coins have the power to save a person's life? Why is *tzedaka* such an incredible connector of community consciousness with life, blessing, abundance, and goodness?

To begin with, *tzedaka* is really not charity. Charity is doing something you don't have to do because you are being nice. You don't feel an obligation to give, but you want to be nice, so you'll give a few coins. That's not really *tzedaka*.

Tzedaka really means "justice." According to justice, you must help someone who has less than you. It's not giving because you feel like giving and want to think of yourself as sweet and generous. *Tzedaka is an obligation.*

By giving out of *tzedaka,* out of justice, we *justify* our existence.

Without giving, there's no reason to exist. Only by being a contributing member of a community do we acquire worth. *Tzedaka* justifies our existence by demonstrating that we are a part of a community in service to a greater reality. At the same time, we recognize that what we are giving is not really our own. It's all Hashem's wealth. We're just passing it on.

As we discussed, the function of consciousness is to acknowledge—in thought, speech, and action—the blessings of life's spiritual wealth and pass them on to the world. And *tzedaka* fulfills that function. We give to each other, because we are all members of a community. Our higher purpose in being part of a community is to acknowledge Hashem as the source of all life and goodness and thereby enjoy the opportunity of being a channel for the presence of Hashem into this world. The simple act of giving *tzedaka* accomplishes that in an instant.

Winston Churchill once said, "We make a living by what we get, we make a life by what we give." *Tzedaka* is not about being nice. *Tzedaka* is about being honest. You are saying, in effect, "It's not my money. It's for me to pass it on. And the more I give away, the more I'm going to get."

Now, if you can't give it away, it's because you think it's yours and that you are the source of your wealth. When you know that it's not yours, that it's only entrusted to you, you have no difficulty in passing it on.

A stingy person is like a wire trying to hold onto electricity. But isn't that crazy? Why would a wire want to hold onto electricity? Its whole purpose is to pass it on, to be a conductor of electricity. That's why a wealthy person is not a person who has a lot. A wealthy person is a person who gives a lot. A person who gives a lot understands that he is plugged into the source of all wealth. Hashem is the source of blessing and wealth. The more conscious a person is of Hashem as the source of wealth, the more he can become a vehicle to channel wealth into the world. But when a person holds onto money, thinking, It's my money, it's just for me, eventually he will lose his wealth. Maybe he won't lose his money literally, but he will lose the blessing of that money. That's why when people who are experiencing financial difficulties seek the advice of a rabbi, often he will tell them, "Give more *tzedaka.*" It may sound odd. Here a person is struggling, unable to make ends meet, and the solution is to give what little he has away? But it works, because by letting it flow out one end, new resources flow into the other end.

I remember a wealthy philanthropist I met in Los Angeles. He told me that when he sold the controlling shares in one of his businesses, he put in the contract that the new owners had to give 10 percent of all earnings to *tzedaka.*

In the contract negotiations the prospective buyers objected, "That's ridiculous! We've never seen anything like this. You can't put that into a contract. You're retaining only a small percentage of the shares. You can't dictate that we give away ten percent of our earnings."

The philanthropist retorted, "If you don't put that into the contract, I won't sell it to you, because you'll destroy my business. The reason I have been blessed with success is that my business is a vehicle for Hashem's wealth to come into the world. As long as it continues to dispense *tzedaka,* I know it's going to continue to receive wealth, because the more it passes it on, the more it gets. I know where all this wealth is coming from."

The buyers decided not to mess with success and accepted his conditions.

A wealthy, very generous man named Joe Berman once told me something that made a deep impression on me. He said, "Very often, when people go through bad times, they ask, 'Why me?' Well, why don't people, when they go through good times, ask, 'Why me?' My whole life, I've been blessed with good times, and I've always asked, 'Why did it come to me? What am I supposed to do with it?' Because I could see that it certainly wasn't coming in just to make me rich."

Very wise advice. We all have to ask ourselves this same question: "Why me? If I have this talent, why me? It's not for myself. If I have this beauty, why me? If I have this money, why me?"

We are each a unique channel for Hashem. Whatever gifts we've been endowed with, our job is to pass them on into the world for others. Therefore, when Torah enjoins us to serve Hashem with joy, it is not talking about some egotistical power that commands, "Serve me, or I'll punish you. And you better do it with a smile!" Rather, if you truly understand that serving as a vehicle for Hashem is the most self-gratifying experience a person can have, of course you will do it joyfully. You will be actualizing what you have been brought into this world to be—a vessel and a vehicle for the presence of Hashem on earth, for the qualities of love and justice and truth and beauty and wisdom, all the qualities of Hashem. So you and others can see Hashem daily.

Another quick connector to the wealth of life is saying blessings.

When I say a blessing over a food, I begin with, "Blessed are You, Hashem . . ." Many people mistakenly think that these words mean that I am blessing Hashem, the Infinite One. But I am in fact acknowledging Hashem as the source of this food. When I eat an apple, I can just eat an apple, or I can, by saying the blessing consciously, make the apple into a conductor wire for channeling Hashem's presence, life force, vitality, goodness, and blessing. An apple can be a nutritious snack, or it can plug me into the source of all life force and nutrition.

When the Israelites were wandering in the desert, Hashem fed them with a hitherto unknown substance called "manna." The people would go out of their tents every morning, and find this strange stuff lying there on the ground. The verse in the Torah introducing the manna says: "I fed you manna—something that you nor your fathers knew what it was—so that you should know that not by bread alone does a person live, but by all that comes from the mouth of Hashem."

Why did it have to be something unfamiliar? What would have happened if the Israelites had woken up in the morning and found bagels all over the place? Imagine being in the middle of the Sinai desert, and every morning bagels appear, sliced in the middle with two centimeters of cream cheese and lox. Now that would be a Jewish experience! Why did it have to be something that didn't look like food?

Because if the manna did look like food, the Israelites would think, Well, okay, the bagels did come from Hashem, the Bagel King, but the nourishment comes from the bagels. However, since the manna obviously could not be nourishing in and of itself, the Israelites would necessarily learn an essential life lesson—all things come from Hashem, not just food, but the nourishment in the food.

The Israelites realized that this odd, gray stuff was not going to nourish them. Hashem was going to nourish them. The manna was just a vehicle for the nourishing love of Hashem. And then they realized that back in Egypt, when they had bread to eat, it was not the bread that nourished them. It was also Hashem.

To the extent that we realize that this bread is a channel for the nourishing energy of Hashem to enter the world, to that extent the bread becomes a channel for the nourishing energy of Hashem to enter the world.

The Kabbalah teaches that if we eat without making a blessing, then the food feeds just our body. It does nothing for our soul. But when we make a blessing on the food, we transform that food. It's not the same bread. It's not the same apple. It's not the same pretzel. The pretzel is no longer a pretzel—it's a vehicle for Hashem's presence to enter the world.

The truth is that all the commandments of the Torah are powerful connectors of consciousness and life—*malhus* and *yesod.* Unfortunately, most people think that the commandments are good deeds that one does. They are more than that. They are deeds that build community consciousness of Hashem and thereby channel Hashem's blessings and goodness into the world. By serving Hashem, I become a vehicle for the life energy to flow into myself and into others. When I serve Hashem it is not self-denial but self-fulfillment, because I am actually serving to manifest the source of all life and thereby I am filled with life. I experience the ultimate joy of personal redemption, a feeling of usefulness and infinite value. And I feel an incredible sensation of freedom and personal liberation, because I feel free to be who I was meant to be.

Having a lot of money doesn't make me feel completely valuable. Giving a lot of money, on the other hand, makes me feel valuable, because I feel that I am serving a higher purpose. This feeling, that I am channeling Hashem's life force, wealth, and blessing into the world, gives me a tremendous sense of worth.

Heaven on Earth

When you look carefully at the story of creation, you see the depiction of all that we have been discussing. The Torah relates: "In the beginning, Hashem created heaven and earth." Note that they were separate, heaven and earth. "And earth was in a state of chaos and emptiness. And there was darkness upon the emptiness." Why?

Because earth was separate from heaven. Earth, which is supposed to be a vessel for heaven, is empty.

When the wire is disconnected from the electricity, the circuit is dead. If the circuit is not connected, the electricity can't flow, and there is no light. Life energy withdraws unless there's a vessel, a vehicle in which it can be channeled into the world. Earth, which was supposed to be full of the transcendental light of heaven, was empty, therefore it dissolved into a state of chaos. Because earth wasn't plugged into heaven, it was dark.

"And the spirit of Hashem hovered over the water." Water is a symbol of instability. Water has no form; it takes the form of whatever vessel contains it. Since earth was not functioning as vessel, everything was fluid, like water. Why was the spirit of Hashem hovering? Because there was no place for the Divine Presence to land, so to speak.

But then the creation story continues. And it is all about how Hashem turns chaos into order by connecting heaven and earth. The climax of the story, of course, is the creation of man.

Man is the one who is going to hold it all together. He is the link between heaven and earth. On the sixth day (or "aeon," according to many explanations), Hashem said, "Let us make man in our image."

Where does the "us" come from all of sudden? According to the Kabbalah, Hashem spoke to all the spiritual and physical components of heaven and earth: "Let us together make man." The human being will be a unique synergy of the physical and the spiritual, a fusion of heaven and earth.

Heaven and earth are connected through Adam. Once Adam is created, what happens? The Torah says, "Heaven and earth and all their hosts were completed."

This, by the way, is why the Kabbalah says Jacob had "the beauty of Adam." One of the ways of understanding Jacob's famous dream of a ladder to heaven is that he dreamed that he himself was the ladder. The ladder had its base on the ground and its top in heaven, and angels, or spiritual energies, were going up and down, down and up. Jacob was the connection between earth and heaven.

That's what a human being is supposed to be. With one's feet on the ground and one's head in heaven, a human being is supposed to be a connector, plugging the physical into the spiritual—a wire through which life energy, Divine energy, can flow.

We can choose to be either a circuit breaker or a circuit maker, depending on how well we devote ourselves to building a global community with a consciousness of working to channel Hashem's life and goodness into the world.

SEEING EXERCISES

1. Can you think of three people you know who embody life and zest? What is it about them that enables them to do that?
2. Which of your activities help you tap into the life force? And which cut you off from that energy?
3. Close your eyes and picture yourself as blessed. What do you see?
4. When do you feel the most connected? What can you do daily to maintain that connection?
5. What have you done in your life to improve the world? What can you do today to improve the world and make it a more blessed place?
6. Who do you know that is the most spiritually connected? What has this person done to accomplish that?
7. Is there someone you know in whose presence you feel spiritually charged? If you cannot think of anyone, how could you find such a person?
8. Is there someone you know in whose presence you feel spiritually drained? What can you do to help change them?
9. Which unique blessings can you personally channel into the world?
10. Which divine quality is the easiest for you to channel? Which quality is most difficult for you to channel?

six

PERFECT HARMONY

Do you remember the old movie musicals where all of a sudden everybody waiting for a subway train starts dancing and singing in perfect harmony? Maybe it isn't as much a fantasy as you think.

To see the perfect divine harmony in life we need to explore in detail the next two sefirot: *netzah* and *hod.*

Netzah literally means "eternity," suggesting staying power, stamina, endurance. It also means "to conquer, to maneuver, to manipulate," which conveys power, triumph and victory. When you add it all up, the one word that most closely approximates *netzah* is "mastery." When we see Hashem's mastery, we feel overwhelmed and retreat in awe.

Hod literally means "glory, beauty, grandeur," but those translations don't convey the real meaning of the word, which is closer to "resplendent glory," "enchanting beauty," "spellbinding grandeur." The one word that I feel best approximates *hod* is "magnificence." When we see Hashem's magnificence, we feel a magnetic attraction and are impelled to draw close in love and admiration. Filled with appreciation, we are inspired to praise and give thanks.

We're going to deal with these two qualities together because they balance each other, like yin and yang. They must manifest in equilibrium; too little of one results in too much of the other.

Just like in any relationship, there is a dialectical dynamic—on the one hand, there is an attraction, an urge to merge, and on the other hand there is the urge to retreat, to maintain one's distinct identity, establish boundaries and borders. So too in our relationship to Hashem, for it to be meaningful, there must be a balance between the attraction and resistance.

When we look at reality through the lenses of Divine mastery and magnificence, we see Hashem in nature and also in the design of our lives.

The more sensitive we become to mastery and magnificence, the more we realize that everything that happens is strategically planned and directed by Hashem. Life is a great drama, and Hashem is the producer and the director. Every scene is perfectly designed and perfectly placed.

The word *netzah* is also related to the word for "orchestra conductor." We begin to recognize that there is a conductor to all of creation, to all of history. And we begin to see Hashem as the maestro and ourselves as members of the philharmonic, playing magnificent masterpieces.

Hashem is the director of the play and we are cast members in the drama. Hashem is the author and we're characters in the story. And everything we see around us are really props on the set. Everyone we meet is also playing a role. Looking at the world in this way is called seeing "Divine Providence."

Providence

The more we open the eyes of our souls to seeing mastery and magnificence, the more we become vehicles for channeling Divine Providence into our world.

What exactly is Divine Providence?

The word "providence" comes from the Latin word *providēre, pro* meaning "before," and *vidēre* meaning "to see." Providence means that everything that is happening has been orchestrated with foresight. What's happening now must take place because of what is predestined. Often it's hard for us to appreciate this until we see what happens later.

This is one of the interpretations of an incredible encounter in the Torah. Moses requests of Hashem, "I want to see Your glory." Hashem replies, "You cannot see My face. You can only see My back."

Of course, the Kabbalistic meaning of this whole mystical episode is far beyond us, but on a simple level we learn that we can see Hashem only after He has passed by us. We can't see Hashem's face—meaning in the present—as Hashem directs our life. But afterward, looking back, we can often see the hand of Providence. By what unfolds in our lives today, we can sometimes recognize how Hashem directed our life yesterday or a year ago or a decade ago. That is seeing Hashem from the back. We are able to appreciate Hashem's foresight in our hindsight.

When something negative happens, we may feel dejected, but then events end up playing out in such a way that suddenly we look back and realize, "My gosh! Everything had to happen as it did so that this could happen! Everything was so incredibly planned, so masterful and magnificent."

I knew a couple, named Larry and Ruth, who tried for years to have a child and finally gave up and adopted. Unfortunately, the child they adopted had major health problems that necessitated getting her chest X-rayed every six months. When this child was about six years old, Ruth finally succeeded in giving birth to her own baby, whom they named Amy. Their joy knew no bounds. The only shadow in their life was their adopted child's health problems. When Amy was eighteen months old, Ruth took the older child for her routine chest X ray. The baby had been coughing, so Ruth thought, As long as I have Amy right here in the X-ray department, I might as well have them X-ray Amy's chest too. The X ray showed that Amy was suffering from the very early stages of cancer. Because they caught it so early, they were able to save Amy's life. Their adopted child's health problems had the positive effect of saving Amy's life. This is Divine Providence. It can only be seen in hindsight.

Explaining this idea, the Talmud tells us the story of Rabbi Akiva and what happened during one of his journeys. Rabbi Akiva was traveling to a far-off place, but when he arrived he found he could not rent a room and had to camp outside of town in some degree of discomfort. However, he said, "This too is for the good. Everything that happens has a reason." He made his camp in the forest together with his donkey and rooster and lit a candle so he could read some holy texts. Shortly, both the donkey and rooster were eaten by wild animals and a strong wind blew out his candle. Not understanding why this misfortune had befallen him, he nevertheless repeated, "This too is for the good. Everything that happens has a reason." In the morning when he once again made his way into the town, he learned how true his statement was. During the night the town had been raided by robbers, and many townspeople had been killed or taken into captivity. He realized that his animals would have made noise and attracted the robbers' attention, and his candle shining in the darkness would have given away the location of his camp. Thus his misfortunes during the night in fact saved his life. All that happened was for the good.

We can all think of a difficult time in life that looking back at it now, was actually a gift. Perhaps you grew from the challenge, or perhaps events conspired to produce a truly positive, unforeseen outcome. Most people can relate stories of losing a job only to find a much better one, or suffering a disappointment that through a chain of circumstances, deposited them in the place where they met the person who was to become their spouse. If we can see the Divine Providence in such twists and turns, we are actually seeing Hashem's back. Looking back, we're able to see how much Hashem looked forward. That's Providence.

Once I was teaching this concept to a seminar group, and I asked the students to share examples of Providence in their own lives. One woman related how the worst period of her life was the nine months she was pregnant with the child of a man she did not marry and did not love. She did not want that baby and spent the entire pregnancy angry and cursing her fate. She considered abortion, and then decided instead to have the baby and give it up for adoption. When the baby was born, she took one look at his face, and she never felt so much joy and love. She now says, "My son has turned out to be the greatest blessing in my life."

That's the consciousness of *netzah* and *hod*. Hashem is directing everything, and much better than we could ever imagine. This is true whether we acknowledge it or not. The only difference is what you choose to see. If you choose to see chaos that's what will be apparent to you; if you choose to see Divine Providence, you won't take a step without realizing how intricately orchestrated the world is.

Playing Our Roles

I once read a book about an author who decides to introduce himself to his character. His character is sitting in a bar, enjoying himself, when all of a sudden the author walks into the bar and looks at him with an expression of familiarity. The character says, "Do I know you, buddy?"

"Do you know me? Of course you know me."

"No, I don't know you," the character says, rebuffing him.

So the author takes out of his pocket a pen and says, "I wrote you."

"What do you mean you wrote me?"

"I wrote you. I wrote you sitting in this bar. I wrote you holding that martini. I'm your author."

And the character jumps up and runs out of the bar. He can't deal with it. He runs away until he's sure he's lost that nut. Then he sits down under a tree, feeling relieved. Sure enough, the author, waving his pen, comes running up to him. The whole story is about a character running away from his author.

Most of us, unfortunately, are like this character—utterly abashed at the idea that we are not self-existent. Most of us think that we are the writer, producer, and director of the show.

When you develop an eye for Divine mastery and magnificence, you look at life's unfolding scenes, and you see a director. You look at gazelles leaping, and you see a choreographer. You look at trees or at flowers and you see an artist; every creation is a masterpiece, reflecting its Master.

That's what the psalms of King David are all about. All the psalms were inspired by the lens of *netzah* and *hod*. King David looked at the wonders of nature and at the tumultuous events of his own life, and he saw a symphony with Hashem as the conductor. He heard a concert. Many of his psalms begin with the words, "A song to the Chief Musician by David."

Of course, as mentioned earlier, *netzah* shares the root in Hebrew with "orchestra conductor," or "chief musician," if you prefer. Hashem is the chief musician, and all of his creation—the people, the roses, the leopards—are his notes, which He is playing. And they all fit together in a great, harmonious symphony.

We all think we're playing solos. In truth, we're all part of one symphony. Most of the time, we are totally unaware of how our lives impact indirectly on the lives of everybody else. You go home happy that you landed that great new job, totally unaware that the person who didn't get it will now undergo a major life transition. You design one of a dozen rings for a jewelry chain totally unaware that one of them will be just exactly what one man had been looking for for thirty years to give his wife. We are all enlisted, whether we knew it or not, into the legions of Hashem. We are all musicians in Hashem's orchestra, dancers in Hashem's chorus line, players on Hashem's team, actors in Hashem's drama. All with a mission, all with a role, all with a part. The only difference is some of us see it, live it, breathe it, and are in a constant state of marvel and wonder, and others are in denial, preferring to live in chaos.

Nothing Is Superfluous

At the completion of the creation story, the Torah relates: "Heaven and earth were finished, and all their legions." The Midrash asks, "What are these legions?" And it answers, "Everything." Everything and everyone in this world has a mission, every worm, every ant, every bird, every animal, and most certainly every human being has a mission, a purpose.

A leaf, for example, may have a specific nourishing or medicinal power. Can we doubt it when we learn that penicillin is nothing more than bread mold? Who would have thought, looking at a humble piece of mold, that it has the power to save lives? But that is its assignment, or some small part of its assignment that we have thus far discovered.

Nothing is superfluous. Even flies and gnats and mosquitoes have a purpose in the cosmic army. According to the Talmud, the great enemy of the Jewish people, Titus, who destroyed the Second Temple, was killed by a tiny fly. This fly flew up his nose, somehow entered his cranial cavity, bore into his brain, and killed him. That fly was on a mission from Hashem.

On an everyday level, the more scientists study ecology, the more interconnections they discover: how if we eliminate a single subspecies, the whole ecosystem goes out of balance and everything in it suffers, because everything has a purpose. That holistic recognition is *netzah* and *hod.*

When we look at nature through the lens of *netzah* and *hod,* we can't help but see a plan and purpose. It's not just a bunch of flies and snakes and trees and flowers and clouds and people and events. Rather, it is an intricately orchestrated symphony, with a virtuoso conductor. Every snake and tree and cloud is poised, waiting for its cue to play its part.

Another amazing story from the Talmud illustrates this idea. Rabbi Isaac Bar-Eliezer was walking with his students along the cliffs of Caesarea during the Roman occupation of Israel when he saw the thigh bone of a large animal roll out from behind a rock. He said, "This is really dangerous." So he picked it up off the path and put it back behind the rock. It rolled out again. "This is very strange," he said, and put it right back in. It rolled out again. "This thigh bone is on a mission," he pronounced to his students. In the distance, they saw a Roman messenger and decided to hide behind some trees and see what would happen. Now, during this period of the Roman occupation in Israel, messages from Rome were generally not good news for the Jews. They watched the runner draw closer, and sure enough, he tripped over the thigh bone, took a blow to his head, and died. Rabbi Isaac and his students then came out of hiding, opened up the runner's pouch, and in it they found a decree to massacre the Jews of Caesarea.

Everything is on a mission. There are no accidents. There is perfect design, perfect order, perfect direction. Every event fits into a grand plot, like in one of those thousand-page novels where something insignificant happens on page 23, and three generations and nine hundred pages later the entire dynasty is saved by the result of that event.

There are countless true examples of this throughout history. My favorite is the biblical Book of Esther where a beautiful young girl is chosen against her will to be the queen. Her encounters with the king are tantamount to rape and you would think that her whole life is one horrible waste. But then, because she is queen, she finds herself in a position to save the entire Jewish population living in Persia from genocide. Her dreadful fate turns into an incredible opportunity for heroism. Her actions become a turning point in Jewish history; she is immortalized in the Bible and remembered every year during the holiday of Purim.

Inspired and Overwhelmed

Kant said that two things fill the mind with ever-increasing admiration and awe the more often one reflects on them: the starry heavens above and the moral law within. When we reflect upon the starry heavens above, we cannot help but feel overwhelmed by the breathtaking mastery of creation and inspired and uplifted by its enchanting beauty.

This is exactly the message of the Jewish evening prayer:

> Blessed are You, Hashem, our Lord, King of the universe, Who by His word brings on evening, with wisdom opens gates, with understanding alters periods, changes the seasons, and orders the stars in their heavenly constellations as He wills. He creates day and night, removing light before darkness and darkness before light. He causes day to pass, and brings night, and separates between day and night. Hashem, Master of Legions is His name.

When we look through the lenses of *netzah* and *hod,* we meet the Master of legions, and we realize that everything is a part of His legions. We stand in awe of the created world, in awe of the sunset and the sunrise and the stars coming out and the moon waxing and waning and the constellations turning with the seasons.

When I'm standing in wonder beside the Grand Canyon, is it this hole in the ground that amazes me? No, it's Hashem's grandeur, Hashem's glory, Hashem's mastery. When I feel inspired to praise or feel filled with gratitude, to whom are all these emotions directed? When I'm awestruck, when I'm taken aback, am I feeling overwhelmed by the power of this pit? No, it's the Master of Legions, Who is manifesting through the Grand Canyon.

I can't intellectually persuade you of any of this. I can only give you properly refracted lenses and hope you will look through them. You have to see Hashem in the world around you and in your life.

When you look through the lens of *netzah* and *hod,* you will see Hashem as the source and power in nature, and the source and power behind your own personal history and world history.

And when you do, you will feel a mixture of awe and gratitude.

The great eleventh-century Jewish philosopher Maimonides wrote: "When a person ponders His great and wondrous works and creations, he immediately loves, praises, and extols, and is filled with great desire to know the Supreme Being."

When I look at the great wonders of creation and feel filled with inspiration, warmed with emotions of love, uplifted with gratitude, then I know I've seen *hod*—Hashem's enchanting magnificence. And I feel a yearning to come close to the source of all this.

On the other hand, when I contemplate these wonders of nature, I also feel overwhelmed with great reverence, stunned by the sheer immensity of the vast universe, and I draw back. That means I saw *netzah*.

Together these two dialectic perspectives create an electric tension that approaches ecstasy.

One of the commandments of the Torah is to love Hashem. How can human beings fulfill that commandment? Maimonides says that the way to love Hashem is by contemplating the wonders of nature. Human beings can encounter Hashem through nature, as the source and the power and the context behind and within nature. Love of Hashem is defined by our sages not as the love of an object in the ordinary sense, but rather as an inner yearning and longing for the source of all knowledge and perfection. Where did all this come from? Where does grandeur come from? Where does splendor come from?

Imagine looking at a very intricate flower, say an orchid. You observe its gorgeous colors and its unique form. Perhaps you smell its fragrance. You feel gratitude for the gift of such resplendent beauty. You say, "This flower is amazing!" And you are drawn to the source of that beauty. You feel love for Hashem, Who cared enough to put orchids into His world.

Then you spend a few more minutes contemplating this orchid.

Its intricate shape is engineered in such a way that when a bee enters the well to get the nectar, certain parts of the orchid move and cause the anthers to dust a bit of pollen onto the anterior of the bee, so when the bee flies away toward the next flower, it is on a mission of cross-pollination. You notice that if the anthers had been a fraction of a millimeter shorter or longer, this carefully engineered pollination system would not have worked. So you feel awed by the infinite Divine mastery that created this astounding orchid. You retreat, overwhelmed.

To see *netzah* and *hod,* you have to open your eyes to the overwhelming power and enchanting beauty of nature, the breathtaking mastery and inspirational magnificence of creation. And then you will be filled with an ecstatic rush of awe and admiration, reverence and love.

Seeing and Responding

Contemplation of nature is a powerful exercise, so powerful, in fact, that it was the path to prophecy in ancient times.

A verse in Psalms declares: "The voice of Hashem is in the water, the voice of Hashem is in the earth." When you are in a forest, do you hear water trickling? Do you hear birds singing? Do you hear bees humming? Or do you hear the voice of Hashem? It depends on your level of consciousness, your awareness of allness, and how sensitive you are to the voice of Hashem as He speaks through nature.

The prophets not only heard the voice, but they also understood the words. For most of us, however, it is a miraculous experience of love and connection to even hear the voice.

Imagine you love somebody very much and she goes on a trip to

Thailand. One day she calls you on a cellular phone, and the connection is really bad. So you can't make out what she is saying. But just hearing her voice makes you feel so close.

According to Kabbalah, the prophets opened themselves up to the Divine voice through meditation on the wonders of nature, through the awareness of *hod* and *netzah,* the beauty and the power, feeling the love and the awe. Of course, they were not in love with nature, but with the Ultimate Reality, Who is manifested through nature and history.

Albert Einstein wrote: "Everyone who is seriously involved in the pursuit of science becomes convinced that a spirit is manifest in the laws of the universe. A spirit vastly superior to that of man, and one in the face of which we, with all our modest powers, must feel humble."

Einstein, who is generally recognized as the greatest scientist who ever lived, experienced a religious emotion that he felt was at the root of all science.

"The finest emotion of which we are capable is the mystic emotion. Herein lies the germ of all art, and all true science. To know that what is impenetrable for us really exists and manifests itself as the highest wisdom and the most radiant beauty, whose gross forms alone are intelligible to our poor faculties. This knowledge, this feeling, that is the core of the true religious sentiment. In this sense, I consider myself among the profoundly religious men."

The prophet, scientist, and artist all want to plug into the source of all creativity, the source of all beauty, power, and life. They are yearning to connect. They don't think that the flower is the source of its beauty, power, or life. They yearn to connect to the true source. Based on this yearning, Einstein said he wanted to form a cosmic religion, but he was too late, because Moses did it before him.

What then is the difference between Einstein and a truly religious person? What is the difference between the scientist's experience of nature and the prophet's? The difference is the distinction between an experience of nature and an encounter with Hashem.

Encounter describes a relationship. When we encounter Hashem through the beauty of nature, we enter into a relationship with Hashem. And relationship implies responsibility. We feel a profound sense of responsibility, which literally is the ability to respond. We feel a call and a willingness to do something.

Imagine two artists hiking through a forest to appreciate nature. How can you tell the difference between the artist who's having an experience and the artist who's in an encounter? The one who's having an experience is awed by the power and appreciates the beauty; he takes a whole roll of photographs and leaves his empty, nonbiodegradable film canister there on the ground where it fell. Because it was his experience, he owned it. The second artist, who encounters Hashem in nature, is inspired to pick up his litter and everyone else's, because it's Hashem's forest, and he feels a responsibility to take care of it. He has entered into a relationship, and he hears a call to duty and responds by cleaning up the forest. When we have an encounter, we're inspired to enlist in the legions of Hashem.

Sure, lots of people out there are enjoying nature. But are they encountering Hashem? They're enjoying the beautiful songs of the birds, but are they hearing the voice of Hashem? If they did, they would know that the voice is calling, inviting a relationship, expecting a response.

Those of us who feel a call to duty are inspired by the understanding that everything and everyone in nature has a post, is strategically placed. We too want to be strategically placed. Our response to Hashem's call is: "How do I enlist? What can I do?"

To Experience or to Encounter

I recall a story someone once told me about Jewish philosopher Martin Buber that illustrates the difference between experience and encounter. A tragic event gave him a clear understanding of the difference between experiencing another person as an object and encountering a person in a relationship. Buber tells the story of the turning point in his life. He was seriously involved with spirituality, mysticism, and meditation. One day, he was meditating in his room, and he entered into an incredible state of mystical ecstasy. Suddenly he heard a knock at the door. He was so high, he wasn't sure he had heard it right, so he waited a few moments. Again, he heard the knock at the door. Buber had to tear himself away from his ecstatic experience in order to answer the door. He opened the door and saw a fellow he didn't know, a stranger. Of course if Buber had had *malhus* consciousness, he wouldn't have perceived anyone to be a stranger. But, he relates, he stood there looking at this stranger who obviously wanted something.

Now, perhaps you've had the experience of dropping in on someone, and when he or she opens the door, you realize, "Oh my gosh, I came at the wrong time." You feel awkward. Just so, this fellow realized he was interrupting Buber, and he felt really awkward. Of course, if he had had *netzah-hod* consciousness, he would have known that there's no such thing as bad timing. Everything is perfectly timed. In any case, he said, "I'm sorry, Mr. Buber, I must be disturbing you. Let me come back another time."

Buber, being a gentleman, said, "No, please, come in, it's fine."

So Buber let him in and had him sit down in his salon and tried very hard to listen and to focus on what his visitor had to say, but most of his mind was still absorbed in the high he had just experienced. The visitor stuttered and stammered and obviously did not feel comfortable sharing with Martin Buber what was on his mind or in his heart. Finally, the fellow apologized, excused himself, and left. And Buber returned to his room and tried to get back into his ecstatic state of consciousness.

Later, Buber heard that this fellow had killed himself. Buber was devastated. He realized that the man had come to him because he desperately needed help, and Buber wasn't there for him because he was so absorbed in his spiritual experience. That's when Buber realized how fake a mystical high can be. If it doesn't open one up to hearing the call to duty, if it doesn't increase one's ability to respond, it is an empty experience.

Many people want to have a so-called God experience. The name for that is spiritual materialism. Just as some people like to amass cars, clothes, and big houses, other people like to amass spiritual experiences. But that's not what a relationship with Hashem is all about.

A true encounter with Hashem means seeing, hearing, and responding to Hashem in your life. In Hebrew this is called *teshuva,* a word often mistranslated as "repentance," but really meaning "answer." To do *teshuva* is to answer Hashem's call.

In that light, we can understand the oft-used biblical expression, "stiff-necked people." What's a stiff-necked person? Someone who, when called, does not turn to listen, just keeps going. *Teshuva* means turning to say, "Yes, I'm here. What can I do for you?"

In the stories of the Torah, Hashem initiates a dialogue with Abraham by calling, "Abraham, Abraham," and then waiting for Abraham to respond, "*Hineni.* Here I am."

That's *teshuva,* turning to hear the call and to respond to it. When I look at nature, I realize that everything's on call. Everyone in this world is on call. And every event is purposely designed as a scene within the drama of life.

True Sensationalism

In this generation, we have moved so far away from *netzah-hod* sensitivity that we have become gluttons for its opposite: sensationalism. Sensationalism means that we have actually become *insensitive* to our senses, so that we have to search for bizarre, grandiose ways of being moved.

When I was a teenager, I was very attracted to rock concerts. I thought I had spiritual experiences at these rock concerts. One of my favorite rock stars was Alice Cooper, who did the most grotesque things on stage. He would come out and do a song with a live cobra around his body. Then he would take a baby doll out of his pocket and sing a song called "Dead Babies." He would hatchet this baby doll into pieces on stage and kick it into the audience while people jumped over each other to get a piece. They paid fifty dollars to be in the front row so they could catch a piece of splintered doll from this crazy rock star. After that, he would take a watermelon and crash it onto the stage and kick the pieces at the audience. Imagine paying fifty dollars for someone to kick watermelon in your face. But people were elated. The finale of the concert was the band hanging Alice Cooper right there on stage. The orchestration would reach a crescendo as they put the noose around his neck and pulled the chair on which he was standing out from beneath him. Then, all of a sudden, the entire stage would go dark and this piercing spotlight would light up his face, which really looked dead. Then the stage would go dark again, and when the lights went back up, Alice Cooper would be dancing in a white tuxedo. The thousands of people in the stadium would be jumping out of their seats, wild, awed.

Sensationalism is supposed to arouse our senses. But it actually does the opposite. It desensitizes us, so that the next concert or movie has to be more gory, more disgusting in order for us to register any response at all. Remember the movie *Bonnie and Clyde*? In its time, it was sensational to see the blood trickling down behind the bushes and to see the blood stains on Bonnie's white dress. That would never work today. No, people want to see the bullet in slow motion going through the victim's forehead, splattering brains all over the screen.

But what are people really looking for?

Netzah and *hod.*

We yearn for the experience of being overwhelmed, retreating back in awe, feeling stunned in the face of the vast and breathtaking. And, at the same time, we long for the experience of admiration, attraction, inspiration and appreciation.

But when we lose our ability to see *netzah* and *hod,* we look for crazy, counterfeit ways to simulate those sensations. Of course, it doesn't work, because sensationalism makes us less sensitive, not more sensitive. It certainly does not inspire responsibility.

What does work? Certainly you won't get it at a rock concert or a thriller movie. And you are not going to go to the Grand Canyon every day. If you want to resensitize yourself to the wonders of nature, learn to see the Grand Canyon in an apple, in a tulip, in a sparrow. It's there; all you have to do is open your eyes to see it.

When you hold your apple at lunch today, consider that Hashem, who encompasses all reality, made this compact, beautiful, colorful, perfectly packaged object that can nourish you with a wealth of vitamins and minerals, all in perfect proportion. That this apple can metamorphose into your brain cells and your muscle cells and your pancreas cells—that's amazing. When you pause to be conscious of it, you're amazed and you're grateful. You take nothing for granted, because you realize that everything's been perfectly designed for your benefit. Then you live in a whole different world.

True sensationalism is the ability to see heaven crammed into a grain of sand. And it doesn't take a prophet to see it. We can all see that vast superior spirit, that all-embracing, ultimate reality that is peering through nature and history and calling to us through every creature and every plant, through every person we meet, every situation we find ourselves in.

SEEING EXERCISES

1. Close your eyes and imagine three different pictures of "mastery." Let one be a picture from a natural setting where you witness the manifestation of "mastery." Let another be a picture from the animal kingdom. And lastly, picture a person you have met who really embodied "mastery."
2. Close your eyes and imagine three different pictures of "magnificence." Again pick one from a natural setting, one from the animal kingdom, and for the last, choose a person who embodied this quality.
3. When I was a kid, we would play a game called I spy. We'd take turns telling the other players: "I spy with my little eye something that is . . . [for example, brown]." Then everybody would look around and try to guess what it was. Play this game with the divine colors. Look for mastery and magnificence. Learn to see these spiritual qualities everywhere.
4. Can you remember three events in your life that you can see in hindsight were Hashem's perfect foresight?
5. Can you think of an event in your life that angered you but see now was really a gift to be thankful for?
6. Think of three difficult situations that are happening in your life now. Can you say for each one: "This is for the good?"

7. Can you think of a stranger you met for only a brief moment who actually changed the direction of your life?
8. Next time you are sitting in a public place, try to imagine that each and every person is playing a unique role on the stage of life and that all are part of one scene at this moment directed by Hashem.
9. Nothing is superfluous. Can you remember something in your life that you almost threw away and that later turned out to be the very thing you needed?
10. Can you remember a time when you were struck with such awe and admiration for the mastery and magnificence of the world that you felt a sense of responsibility? What did you do?
11. Can you give a personal example of your experience with sensationalism and another of the true joy of sensation?

seven

LOVE IN THE BALANCE

Next we are going to look at another pair of *sefirot* that function in harmony—*gevurah,* which means "strength" in the sense of restraint, discipline, judgment, law and order, and *hesed,* which means "kindness, generosity."

When we look at reality through the lenses of *netzah,* mastery, and *hod,* magnificence, we see Hashem in and through nature and history as the source of, and the power behind, these manifestations. But when we look at reality through the lenses of *gevurah* and *hesed,* we see Hashem as the source and the power behind morality and ethics.

When we look at the world through the lens of *gevurah,* we see borders, boundaries, law and order. In short, we see judgment. When we look through the lens of lawfulness and borders and boundaries, we come to understand that there are rules in the world and that when we violate these rules, there are bound to be consequences. When we look at the world in that way, then we see Hashem as judge.

If I am walking down the street and I trip and fall and I ask, "Why me?" I just tasted judgment and its natural consequence justice. Why would I ask, "Why me?" Because I have a certain sense that there are consequences, that things happen for a reason. That I get what I deserve.

Now, if I get angry when what happens seems unfair, that is also a taste of *gevurah.* After all, why would I get angry? If I did not inherently perceive the world as conforming to a set of moral rules, why would I even ask why bad things happen to good people?

Human beings have an innate sense of justice. When something happens that doesn't seem to be expressing justice, we get angry. That anger itself is an awareness of Hashem as judge. We're wondering why Hashem isn't being revealed in the world as a fair judge.

The opposite is also true. We feel good when we watch a movie in which the bad guy gets his just desserts in the end, and when the good guy gets well-earned recognition. I would wager that almost everybody in the world was happy when Mother Teresa got the Nobel Peace Prize. Why? Because human beings instinctively rejoice when goodness is rewarded. We love the taste of justice, and we recognize Hashem as a judge.

According to the Kabbalah, the creation of the world is associated with the attribute of *gevurah,* law and order, judgment. What does creativity have to do with judgment? Both creativity and judgment express the ability to know where to draw the line, get things in line, and keep things in line. That's how the world is structured. Without that structure, the world wouldn't be—there would only be chaos.

Game Rules

A Midrashic story relates that when Hashem created the world, every creature was told what it would eat, how it would survive, to whom it would be subordinate, and who would be subordinate to it. Every creature, including human beings, was told this specifically. And every creature accepted these rules of engagement with joy. Every creature said, "Yes, I accept those terms."

The Midrash is trying to tell us that when we came into this world, we accepted the game rules. We accepted the limitations that were placed on us and the role that we were assigned to play. And by accepting that role, we became accountable, so that means we are now liable if we violate the terms of the agreement.

We have no excuses. Everything had been explained to us beforehand. The rules were read out loud, we were cautioned, and we went forward to fulfill our mission with open eyes.

If this was not so, we would not be responsible for our actions. According to Torah law, a person cannot be punished for a crime unless he had been warned not to commit the act. Even if a person commits a murder in front of witnesses, he is not liable for the death penalty unless someone said to him beforehand, "You know, murder is wrong." And the murderer had to have heard the warning and responded, "Yes, I know it's wrong, but I'm going to do it anyway."

The Midrash is reminding us that within us we know there is a right and a wrong—there are rules. We have been cautioned and we have accepted. We are accountable.

So before Hashem could create the world and bring us into this world, He had to, so to speak, notify us of the game rules. If there are no game rules, there is no game. If there is no right and wrong, then what difference does it make what I do? If there is nothing to violate, there is nothing to fulfill. I can't even play a game of basketball without rules, let alone live my life!

Recently a friend asked me if I would meet with his son, Sam, and help him prepare his bar mitzvah speech. I generally don't teach thirteen-year-olds, but for my friend I made an exception. I met with Sam and began to share with him some of my insights into the Torah portion he would be reading in the synagogue on Shabbat. I really got deep into the mystical meanings behind the passages he would be reading and Sam seemed to be understanding me. I was very impressed, but after about an hour, I asked him, "Do you have any questions?"

Sam said, "Yeah, just one. Why do I have to obey all these commandments and keep all these rules?"

Well, I felt pretty silly. Here I was going off the deep end when he didn't even know what his bar mitzvah meant.

I asked him, "Do you like football?"

"I love it!" Sam exclaimed. "I play it all the time."

"Do you know the rules?"

"Of course; you can't play if you don't know the rules."

"Why not?"

" 'Cause then there would be no game. You couldn't win or lose. There couldn't be touchdowns, no out-of-bounds, no violations, no penalties. Without the rules it would just be a bunch of people running around. It would be a mess and it would be no fun."

"Precisely, and that's true about the game of life also. Without rules and regulations it would be a mess, no fun, no adventure, no challenge. And even though we all know that it's not whether you win or lose, but how you play the game, without those rules there would be no way to evaluate how you play the game. The Torah's commandments are the game rules of life and Hashem is the referee."

In the end, Sammy got psyched for his bar mitzvah.

Truth or Consequences

If your soul has seen the quality of lawfulness and judgment, *gevurah,* then you have seen that reality is a judge.

This is the root for the feeling of fear. We're not afraid of Hashem; we're afraid of losing what we have. There's no reason to be afraid of the judge. Rather, you are afraid that his verdict might cost you a $10,000 fine.

Imagine you are a contestant on a television game show. You've been on the show three weeks straight, and you've accumulated $245,000 in prizes. The host offers you one more question, for double or nothing. You decide to go for it. He asks the question, and you answer to the best of your ability. He is standing there, looking at the card with the correct answer. What you feel at that moment is fear. You're not afraid of the host. You're afraid of losing your $245,000 by giving the wrong answer. It really has nothing to do with the host. You either answered correctly or you didn't. But the host is the one who is going to say, "Right" or "Wrong."

Understanding this point is critical for a healthy relationship with Hashem. We should never fear Hashem. Hashem is not out to get us. Hashem is not like some mean, angry person who reacts because his ego has been challenged. We should only fear the consequences of our choices and actions. And even that fear can be minimized when we remember that paying the consequences is in our best interest and happens only for our spiritual growth. The consequences are necessary to put things back in line, to reestablish balance and restore justice.

Why is it so hard to see justice? Why do we not readily see the consequences of evil acts and good deeds?

When people lived on a higher spiritual level, it was possible to see justice clearly and openly. The Midrash tells us that while the Israelites were wandering in the desert, how far a person had to go to find manna each morning was directly proportional to how he or she had behaved the day before. A person who had behaved righteously would find manna right outside the door of the tent. A person who had behaved wickedly would have to walk very far to find it. Wouldn't it be great if we had that kind of moral feedback system in our lives today?

The quality of justice is hidden in our world because it can only enter into our world if we acknowledge it and embody it through thought, speech, and action. It's an amazing and frightening idea.

It goes back to, Everything is in the hands of Hashem except the awe of Hashem. Hashem's hand is in everything that happens. Hashem takes care of everything. But we must choose to see his handiwork all around us in order to enjoy the ecstasy of feeling Hashem's closeness and presence. Or we can choose not to see and live with that.

Blowing the Fuse

A verse in Deuteronomy states, "You are weakening the Rock that gave birth to you." This is a shocking idea. That we have the power to weaken Hashem in this world. I, a measly mortal, can weaken Hashem? But if I am not acknowledging the qualities of Hashem, then the manifestations of those Divine qualities fade and almost disappear from my world. If I'm not seeking justice and behaving accordingly by embodying justice in the way I behave with others, then I am not allowing justice to flow into this world. Then I, so to speak, am weakening Hashem's presence in this world.

That's what it means to desecrate the Divine name.

In Hebrew, the term for desecrating the Divine name is *hillul*

Hashem. Hillul actually means "to empty out." Therefore, to desecrate the Divine name means to remove Hashem's presence from this world. In contrast, *kiddush Hashem,* a sanctification of the Divine name, means to draw Hashem's presence into the world.

So, our behavior can either be causing an emptying out of Hashem from this world, or our behavior can be filling this world with Hashem. It's up to us to do our part for the world.

A verse in Psalm 106 asks, "Who will speak the *gevurah* of Hashem?" Who will express the justice of Hashem? If no one's out there demanding law and order, justice won't come into this world, and this world will be filled with chaos.

It's important to understand that from our limited human vantage point, which sees less than one percent of the cosmic picture, it appears unjust when a nice person gets sick or a tornado devastates an entire area. This is a subject that would require another whole book, but for now let it suffice to say that in our present state of consciousness, we are not able to see the whole picture of Divine justice. When we get to the next dimension, then we will see the big picture, and we'll see that justice permeates everything, always.

Justice is a quality of reality, whether you see it or not. Your actions and your attitude do not effect reality. Rather, they effect *your* world, or the way Hashem manifests in your world. By acknowledging law and order and embodying them in your thought, speech, and action, through your relationships, your business dealings, the way you conduct your profession, and even by the way you act in a supermarket, you bring justice into this world.

On the other hand, if, every time you walk through the produce section, you help yourself to a handful of grapes, you are driving justice from the world. If the cashier mistakenly gives you change of a $5 bill instead of a $1 bill, and you realize her mistake and say,

"Hey, you gave me too much change," you are bringing justice into the world. You are lighting up the whole supermarket with the presence of Hashem as judge.

Justice Empowers

Who was the first person to really bring justice into the world? The patriarch Isaac, who represents *gevurah.* The Zohar says that people were frightened of Isaac because he went around telling them that there is a judge and that they were going to get what they deserved. People didn't like hearing that.

That's why Isaac didn't have a big following. People don't like to hear about judgment. They don't want to see reality through the lens of law and order and have to acknowledge that Hashem is a judge.

Many people can't understand how Isaac's religion related to his father Abraham's religion, since Abraham taught from the perspective of love and kindness. Isaac, on the other hand, told people, "You're liable, you're accountable, you're going to get what you deserve, because there is cause and effect. There are borders and boundaries. There are choices. There are consequences."

Justice empowers us. If what I do doesn't make a difference, then I don't make a difference. If I can't violate anything, I also can't fulfill anything. If I can't lose, I can't win. If I can't lose the game because there are no rules, then I can't win the game because there are no rules. So justice is critical. It's what empowers us.

Justice tells you that you can make a difference. And what you do is either going to be a violation or a fulfillment. It is either going to hurt this world or help it. And that is empowerment. You might not love it, but it gets people moving.

I remember when, after completing rabbinical studies, I did my compulsory army service, as every Israeli citizen has to do. I was in a special unit for older guys. On the first day, we were all standing at attention when our sergeant walked up to take command. He was no more than nineteen years old. I couldn't believe it. He made this stern, mean face. Not "Welcome to the camp," not even "We're going to have a good time here." He looked at us with this angry face, and he paced back and forth with his hands behind his back, staring at us. Then he yelled, "I don't care if I'm nineteen years old. In the army it's not age, it's rank. I'm a sergeant, and you're just privates."

He paced a couple more minutes, giving us mean looks. Then he yelled, "I want you to know that you're going to do what I say. Because if you don't do what I say, we have ways of punishing you. We have ways of rewarding you too. I'm sure you would like to have time to buy some candy bars and cigarettes, and we'd like you to be able to buy your candy bars and your cigarettes. If you do what we say, we'll give you five minutes in the day to buy what you want. If you don't, no candy bars or cigarettes, boys."

I couldn't believe it. It was the first time I ever wanted to smoke a cigarette. Within minutes he had us moving. We knew that if we performed, we were going to get what we earned. He created a whole system of reward and punishment using perks that had never meant anything to me. All of a sudden, it was, "Come on, guys, let's go, let's go. You want your Nestlé's Crunch!" I ran to the canteen to buy a candy bar, when suddenly I remembered, "I hate chocolate!"

Reward and punishment works. It gets people moving. It was unbelievable how this nineteen-year-old sergeant was able to get fifty guys out of bed within five minutes. I would be sleeping and suddenly I would hear Sergeant Junior shout, "Wake up!" I never got up so fast. There we would be, lined up like a really crack troop, and we would feel tremendous. We were empowered. It's unbelievable what human beings are able to do. Justice and judgment, rules and accountability, reward and punishment really motivate and empower people.

However, if justice is not balanced with kindness, it can destroy people. It can turn them into robots. That's why *gevurah* must be balanced by *hesed.*

When we get a glimpse of justice, we see that Hashem is a judge. On the other hand, when we see kindness, we see that Hashem is a lover.

It's All a Gift

So now, let's examine *hesed.* What do kindness and generosity really mean?

It's the opposite of getting what you deserve. It's realizing that you don't deserve anything. Everything is a gift. Kindness is when you do something you don't have to do.

Let's say I dent your car. I have to pay. If I say to you, "You know what, I'll do you a favor. I'm willing to pay you for the damage," I am way off base. I am doing you no favor at all; it's my obligation to make things right. I am doing the just thing, not the kind thing.

Kindness is when, all of a sudden, I just walk up to your car and start washing it. I don't owe you anything. You've never done anything for me that I need to reciprocate for. I just feel like washing your car. That's *hesed.*

Hesed is gratuitous. *Hesed,* or kindness, is free. I was struck by the spectacular Divine color of *hesed* one day when I was sitting in a park feeling pretty blessed. I was thinking about my children and my wife and my job and my friends and all the things I have. Suddenly, it hit me: I had done nothing to deserve all this. In fact, I couldn't even think of what I *could* do to deserve all this. Is there anything I could have done or could ever do to merit having a child? Is there anything I could ever do to merit my baby's ten toes and ten fingers? Not to mention his circulatory system and his digestive system. How does one deserve a functioning liver? I was overcome with a realization of how everything is totally gratuitous. What I've earned by my efforts doesn't come anywhere close to everything that I've got.

Then another realization hit me: Even a world of rules is a gift. That's why Kabbalah tells us that *hesed* is the root and foundation of *gevurah*. There didn't have to be any game of life or any rules. It's an amazing idea, which explains an odd verse in Psalms, "Hashem you are kind because You pay a person according to their deeds." How can the psalmist call this kindness? Why does he refer to justice as a kindness. What's the kindness of justice? After all, justice is justice. I get what I deserve. But is getting what I deserve something I deserved, or was that also a gift?

It's all a gift. When you realize this you are filled with gratitude. When you realize that nothing had to be, then you have seen kindness and you have seen that Hashem is a lover.

The blessing Jews say before eating bread makes no apparent sense: "Blessed are You Hashem, King of the Universe, who produces bread from the earth." That's ridiculous! Bread doesn't come from the earth. When was the last time you saw bread growing out of the ground, or from a stalk of wheat? I mean, I'm willing to accept that Hashem produces wheat, but human beings produce bread. If you've ever made bread, you know that you have to really sweat over it, mixing it, kneading it. So how can I make a blessing saying that Hashem produced bread?

You see, when I make that blessing on bread, I not only bless it for its nutritional value, I bless the fact that we are able to make bread. Bread is the symbol of human ingenuity, of human effort. That's why money is referred to as bread. The one who works to support the family is called the breadwinner. When I say this blessing and acknowledge that the bread comes from Hashem, I realize that even human ingenuity and human effort are a gift. It's all a gift.

Abraham, One of a Kind

Abraham was the first person to see Hashem as a lover, the source of kindness, the benevolent one. So Abraham became the vehicle and channel for kindness in this world. He gave the world a taste of kindness, and thereby the recognition of Hashem as the ultimate lover and source of all kindness. How did he do it?

He started a free hotel in Beersheba.

There, in the middle of the desert, he provided food, drink, and shelter for every wayfarer who happened by. Abraham's tent had openings on all four sides, so he could see everybody who was passing by in all directions. And he would literally run out to offer them a meal and a rest.

During Abraham's time, the cities of Sodom and Gomorrah, which represented the opposite point of view, thrived. In these cities, which were wealthy, upscale communities, it was illegal to commit acts of kindness. Why give alms to a beggar? What has he done to deserve it? It is only an act of weakness and encourages dependency.

The Torah tells us that when Lot, Abraham's nephew, invited in some strangers (who were really angels disguised as men), a mob gathered outside his door. They were ready to lynch him for violating the rule of the city. What was this rule? "What's mine is mine, and what's yours is yours." If misguided people like the family of Abraham started mixing things up by giving things away gratuitously, then the whole property system would be undermined.

Abraham had challenged the very basis of the pagan worldview. It was not just an issue of one God versus many gods. It was realizing that the foundation and the theme of life is kindness, as it says in Psalm 89: "The world is founded upon *hesed*."

It means that the world does not have to be. You don't have to be, I don't have to be. Everything is expendable. Obviously, if I don't exist, the world is going to go on. Moreover, if the world doesn't exist, reality is going to go on. Hashem will continue to exist. Whether there's a world or not, Hashem will continue to be. The whole world is expendable.

On the one hand, becoming aware of this can make me feel inconsequential, but on the other hand, it can make me feel fantastic because, if this world is gratuitous, then it's a free gift, and I should be gracious and act in kind to others. That is the complete opposite of idolatry, because these idolaters deified the natural world, where only the law of the jungle reigns and where kindness is nonexistent.

Once I was walking through the antiquities section of the Israel Museum, which is full of artifacts from the Canaanite civilization of Abraham's time. In the glass cases I saw dozens of "cult figures," which is a fancy name for idols. I was struck by how many of the idols were in the form of animals. Why would human beings idolize animals? I mean, I can understand why people might worship the sun and the stars; they are vast and majestic. But why would anyone idolize a sheep or a goat?

The pagan world believed that nature is God. Not that nature is a manifestation of God and that whether or not the manifestation exists, God will exist. But in the pagan world, nature was believed to be eternal. It always was, always is, and always will be.

Therefore, all the forces of nature were gods that always were, are, and will be. Each man therefore aspired to merge with nature and be as spontaneous as the animal kingdom, doing what comes naturally.

Abraham was the first person who in effect said that nature is created by a Supreme Nonphysical Reality, Who always is, was, and will be. And this world and nature are only a manifestation of the Creator. Therefore, this created world didn't always exist and didn't have to be; it's a gift. Nature is a totally gratuitous gift. Pomegranates didn't have to be. Sunsets didn't have to be. Shade didn't have to be. The color magenta didn't have to be. It's all a gift. It's all kindness. And therefore, to be in sync with the foundation and theme of life, we too should reflect kindness.

The difference between Abraham and the idolaters was that they believed that you merged with the divine by merging with nature, and he believed that you merged with the divine by transcending nature and becoming one with reality—Hashem.

Giving Freely

Psalm 89 says, "The world is founded on *hesed.*" The laws we see operating in nature are actually subordinate to an even higher principle of reality—kindness.

Once you realize that the natural world was built upon kindness and that the basis of life is kindness, it makes sense to act accordingly, plug into the root of it all, and be kind. It makes sense to give freely to others and to be part of that great flow of giving. Even though kindness does not seem to be the operative principle of nature—what, after all, is kind about the law of the jungle—it is, in fact, the foundation of everything.

Kindness may not be a quality of nature but it is a quality of reality and the foundation of nature. Even if giving freely may not come naturally, even when our inclination is to be selfish, we should transcend our nature, be kind. It might not feel natural, but when we overcome our nature and do kindness we will feel that we are being real, because we will be in sync with reality. Somehow people intuit that it is better to give than take and they feel a deeper joy when they overcome their selfish nature and plug into the selfless reality, Hashem.

In contrast, if we prefer to believe that nature is the ultimate reality, then in our world everything will operate according to the natural law and then the law of the jungle will rule supreme.

In the jungle it makes no sense to give away the food you worked for; all that matters is the survival of the fittest. In the jungle, might makes right and there is no reason to be kind. Can you imagine a lion pouncing on a zebra, then suddenly noticing the baby zebra, and, because the lion realizes that life would be too hard for the baby zebra without its mother, deciding to be kind, and going away hungry? We see kind animals only in Walt Disney movies. According to the laws of nature, it's ridiculous to be kind. If I were in sync with the laws of nature, I would be a sucker to give away my hard-earned money to the homeless, unless there was something in it for me, but then my gift would not be kindness, it would be business.

From the perspective of the idolater this world is not a community, it's a jungle. There is no Creator. There are just warring powers of nature. And when you think you live in a jungle, then you live by the rules of the jungle.

The ethos of the ancient idolatrous world was adopted in modern times by Adolf Hitler. This is what he said:

"In nature there is no pity for the lesser creatures when they are destroyed so that the fittest may survive. Going against nature brings ruin to man . . . It is only Jewish impudence to demand that we overcome 'nature.'"

Abraham was not only kind, he was smart. How did he fight the idolaters' worldview? With kindness.

Whenever a stranger would happen by, Abraham would run to invite him into his free hotel. He would take this stranger, whom he didn't know, and to whom he owed nothing, and lovingly escort him to his tent. Then he would sit him down in the shade, wash his feet to cool him off, bring him water to drink, and serve him a lavish meal.

When the guest said, "Thank you," Abraham, according to the Midrash, responded: "Don't thank me. Thank the One from Whom it has all come."

The idolater wouldn't know what he was talking about. "The food came from you. I'm thanking you."

Abraham would say, "If you don't thank Hashem, then you have to pay me for the meal."

When I first read this story in the Midrash, I thought it was horrible. Abraham sounded like some manipulative missionary. You know, he's nice to you if you buy into his beliefs, but if you don't buy into his beliefs, he slaps you with a bill. He is not really being kind, because he wants something in return.

But many Midrashic stories may seem totally off the wall until you really reflect on them. So I thought about it. And I realized that Abraham was showing those idolaters their own inner contradiction: If you can eat my free meal, then you must accept the concept of giving something for free. But according to the worldview that you subscribe to, it's ridiculous that I should be kind to you. You're a stranger, and I don't owe you anything. Therefore, either stick with your way of seeing the world and give me something in return—that is, pay me for the food you ate—or honestly acknowledge that it's all a gift, that kindness is a quality of reality, and express gratitude to that reality, Who is Hashem.

The sages tell us that the true kindness of Abraham toward these strangers was not the giving of food but the giving of a taste of the divine flavor, of kindness and showing them Hashem. There is no greater gift than the realization that it is all a gift and experiencing the profound joy of thankfulness.

Abraham channeled *hesed* into the world. That's why Abraham is called a *merhava,* which means a chariot or vehicle for Hashem.

Manual for Living

Now let's look at the difference between Abraham and Isaac.

Abraham was willing to help people he didn't have to help. He was willing to do things he didn't have to do. Why? Because he realized that that's the way reality operates. Hashem does things that He doesn't have to do. Hashem didn't have to create the world. Creation was an act of kindness. Therefore, Abraham served Hashem by revealing the divine quality of kindness through doing acts he did not have to do. Abraham's service to Hashem was a labor of love.

No one taught Abraham that he had to serve Hashem. On his own, he realized: "How can I not want to serve Hashem, when I see how much Hashem is serving me? Hashem doesn't owe me anything, and yet Hashem serves me every day. Each breath I take is really a gift." Abraham established the foundation of life—it is loving Hashem.

When Hashem spoke to Abraham for the first time, He said: "Go for yourself to a land that I will show you, and I will bless you, and make you a great nation." It is important to understand that

Hashem didn't command him to go. Hashem suggested he go. The Hebrew words *lekh leha* literally mean, "go for yourself." In other words, "Don't do it for me. I'm just giving you good advice."

So what did Abraham do? The Torah says that Abraham's attitude was: "I don't want to go for myself, I want to go for You. Let me make this journey for You." Abraham, in his love for Hashem, wanted to serve Hashem. For Abraham the greatest gift was to do something for Hashem, the greatest gift was the opportunity to love Hashem.

Isaac, on the other hand, served Hashem out of fear. Not out of fear of Hashem, but out of fear of losing the gift of life and the gift of service. He realized that the gift was gratuitous and that there was nothing he could have done to earn it, but there was something he could do to lose it. The game is a gift, and the rules of the game are a gift. There are rules to follow, and those who violate them could lose the game. Isaac wasn't afraid of Hashem, but he was afraid of losing the gift of life and the gift of connection to Hashem.

I tried to explain this to my son. I said, "Imagine I give you a ball. It's a gift. And I ask you, 'Please don't bounce it in the house.' Wouldn't it be ungrateful for you to take the ball and then bounce it in the house?"

That's essentially the problem. People are walking around in this world thinking, "It's my life and I can do with it as I please." Yes, it is your life, but not because you created it, or earned it. It's a gift and it comes with conditions. Hashem says, "It's your life as long as you abide by the rules. I give you life as a gift, but, please, abide by these particular conditions." It's not because Hashem wants to be mean, but because He knows that if we use this gift in the wrong way, it won't be a gift anymore. It will turn into a curse. If my son bounces the ball in the living room and breaks a lamp, shattering slivers of glass all over the floor and the furniture, then he has turned the gift into a weapon of destruction, and he can't even walk or sit down in the living room anymore without getting cut. I didn't lay down the rule to be mean or to limit his fun. I laid down the rule to protect him from the consequences of misusing the gift.

Torah lays down a lot of rules. If I follow the rules, I enjoy the gift of life in the optimal way it can be enjoyed. People mistakenly think that the rules or commandments of Torah are going to take away their enjoyment of life. It's the opposite. Do the rules take away your enjoyment of baseball or tennis? Of course not.

Imagine someone gives you a Pentium computer and eight or nine state-of-the-art programs. You're thrilled to have this gift, right? Then your benefactor presents you with a pile of thick tomes. "What are these?" you ask?

"These are the rules, the do's and the don'ts," he says. "These are the manuals that teach you how to use Windows, the word processing program, the graphics program, the office manager, the schedule maker, the fax/modem, and the net surfer."

"I don't need all these rules," you might say, throwing away the manuals. So, you sit down and start pressing buttons on the keyboard, and eventually, with online help, you learn how to write letters and save them and call them up and change them, and even how to fax your letters to your friends. "What a great computer I have," you say. But unfortunately, you will never enjoy 95 percent of what the computer is capable of doing.

That's what the Torah's commandments really are—an instruction manual for living. They enable us to use the gift of life to its fullest.

In summary, Hashem's justice preserves the gift that Hashem's kindness bestows. The consequence of abusing life is losing life. Is that a punishment? No, it's a consequence. If you push the wrong combination of buttons on your computer keyboard, and the whole memory is erased, is that a punishment from the CEO of Microsoft? No, it's the consequence of your not using the computer properly.

In reality, there is no such thing as punishment. Not in the sense of Hashem getting back at you. Actions have consequences and those consequences are determined by Hashem's justice. But it is always important to remember that even the consequences determined by justice are themselves rooted in Hashem's kindness. The basic attitude of Torah is that all that happens to a person is in the person's best interest. Hashem is always on your side.

SEEING EXERCISES

1. List instances when you felt Hashem's judgment.
2. List instances when you felt Hashem's kindness.
3. Did you find that one of these lists was easier to write than the other?
4. List ten game rules you follow in your life? How did you develop your game rules?
5. List ten game rules of the person you are closest to in your life. Can you think of two new game rules that would improve your life?
6. Can you remember a time when you were afraid of Hashem when you should have really feared the consequence of your own choice?
7. Can you think of three things that you have done to bring justice into the world? Can you think of one thing you can do today that could bring justice into the world?
8. Take one minute and try to list every gift from Hashem that you have been given.
9. Next time you are sitting idly on a bus or waiting for an appointment, think of every part of your body and thank Hashem for it. Start from the top of your head and work your way to the tips of your toes.
10. Next time you sit down to eat, pause in silence and acknowledge that the food before you is a gift.

11. What are the three greatest acts of kindness that you have done in your life? What act of kindness can you do today?
12. Who is the most just person you know? Who is the kindest person you know?
13. What do you think is the greatest act of kindness anyone could ever do?

eight

FACE-TO-FACE

Beauty is truth, truth beauty.

KEATS, "ODE ON A GRECIAN URN"

The Kabbalah calls the combined quality of beauty and truth *tiferet.* The Kabbalah describes *tiferet* as a clear lens, whereas all the other *sefirot* are referred to as colored lenses. When you see the beauty/truth of Hashem, you are inspired by the awesomeness before you.

According to the Kabbalah, when we encounter the Divine quality of *tiferet,* we intimately connect with the timeless source and context of all being, which is suggested within the meaning of the essential name of Hashem—Y/H/V/H. This is why, to truly understand what we see when we look through the clear lens of beauty/truth, we need to appreciate the meaning of names.

All the other names of Hashem that are associated with the other *sefirot* are titles: Master, Conductor, Supervisor, Creator, Father,

Judge. But the private personal name, the name that evokes a direct encounter, not only with presence but with essence, is Y/H/V/H. This is why *tiferet* is described as a clear lens.

In order to really understand *tiferet,* we have to understand what a name is, and what the difference is between a name and an essential name.

Perhaps you've had the experience of sitting in an airplane next to a stranger. You start up a conversation, talking about work and family. Soon you've been talking for two hours, and you realize that you don't even know his name. There's an awkward hesitation and you finally say, "What's your name?" And he hesitates for a moment, wondering, "Hmm, should I give him my name?" What's the big deal about a name? You have already found out that he's a CEO and an artist and a husband and a father and a son, that he and his wife did six months of marriage counseling, but he's hesitant to tell you his name.

Why do you think this happens? When you tell someone your name, you establish a direct relationship, essence to essence, soul to soul. Everything else you revealed until now—that you are an artist, boss, father, husband, son—added up to titles; they're not your name. They express formal relationships, but not a direct intimate connection.

The Name Game

Imagine that Miss Jones and Mr. Smith are set up on a blind date. They meet at a nice restaurant, and after the initial awkwardness, the conversation begins to flow. After they've had their cocktails, he asks her, "Miss Jones, how long have you lived in the city?" She says, "Please, call me Elizabeth." He smiles and says, "And you call me Robert."

They really like each other, so a couple nights later they go to a movie. On the way home, she asks him, "Robert, what did you think of the film?" He says, "You know, my friends call me Rob." She smiles and says, "My friends call me Liz."

Now they're seeing each other regularly and talking on the phone every day. One evening, during a particularly intimate moment, he confides to her, "My closest friends call me Bobby. I want you to call me Bobby." She kisses him and confides, "My family call me Leelee. I want to be Leelee to you."

Everything is going great for a couple weeks. Then one day Bobby and Leelee are relaxing over the Sunday paper together, and they start talking politics. It turns out that he's an archconservative, and she's a flaming liberal. They start to distance themselves. "Rob," she says in her most strident voice, "I can't believe you think that."

"Liz," he says sitting up straight. "How can someone as intelligent as you buy into that ideology?"

"Any thinking person would come to the same conclusion, Robert," she says icily.

"Well, Elizabeth, I guess I didn't know you as well as I thought I did."

"No, you didn't know me at all, Mr. Smith."

"Miss Jones, you can keep your stupid opinions," he says, slamming the door behind him.

Names denote a relationship. I'm a rabbi, but that's not my name. That's my title. People who have a personal relationship with me call me David. David is the person behind Rabbi. David is indicative of my essential self. Rabbi is the role I play. Rabbi is a garment that I wear. I'm also a father, a son, an employer, and a musician. Those are all garments that I, David, wear. And just like I change my clothing, I change the roles I play. But my essence as David I never change.

My wife told me, after we got engaged, that the whole time we were dating, she never referred to me by my name. In fact, even when she was at home with her family, she would never refer to me by name. I asked her why, and she said, "Because to even say your name implied to me a level of relationship that I wasn't sure I was ready, or you were ready, to have."

Through the clear lens of *tiferet,* associated with the essential name Y/H/V/H, we encounter the Divine essence. Through all the other names, we encounter Hashem's presence, but there's a big difference between presence and essence. Like the difference between seeing the back of your friend's head and seeing his face. When I see the back of my friend's head, I know he is here, I experience his presence. But only when I see his face do we connect and I experience his essence. That's what face-to-face means.

Has anyone ever connected with Hashem face-to-face?

Yes. Moses, his brother, Aaron, and the Israelites, at Mount Sinai.

Most of the people only caught a glimpse, but Moses and his brother had daily face-to-face encounters with Hashem. No one else did. In Exodus, chapter 5, Hashem appears to Moses: "I am Y/H/V/H." Hashem goes on to say: "And I appeared to Abraham, Isaac, and Jacob under the title *El-Shadai,* but My name, Y/H/V/H, I did not make known to them."

This verse shows us a distinction between the patriarchs and Moses in terms of the intensity of the encounter with the Divine. The verse says, "I *appeared*" to the patriarchs, but "I was not *made known*" to them.

What does it mean to make oneself known or to know someone?

The Torah says, "And Adam knew his wife." And we understand that knowing someone in the biblical sense implies a very intimate connection. So there's something about Moses' level of consciousness that brought him to a direct connection with the Divine.

The patriarchs saw Hashem in history and nature. They saw

Hashem's Providence in the ordinary vicissitudes of life. But they never witnessed an outright miracle. Abraham and his servant Eliezer beat great armies all by themselves. That was truly remarkable but it still happened through the natural format of battle. Isaac planted a few seeds and the harvest reaped was mysteriously one hundred times what he planted. That was supernatural but it was still expressed through the natural venue. Moses, however, intimately knew Y/H/V/H, the Divine Who transcends nature.

So Moses' story is replete with miracles, from the ten plagues, to the splitting of the sea, to the daily provision of manna falling from the sky and water gushing from a rock. Moses came to know Hashem in an intimate, direct, face-to-face encounter, not through the guise of nature. The difference between Moses and all other prophets was that Moses was able to see Hashem through the clear lens called *tiferet*. He met Hashem face-to-face and became the vehicle for Torah. The other prophets saw Hashem through the tinted lens of *netzah* and *hod,* through contemplation of the wonders of nature and history. They saw Hashem only from behind. They heard Hashem through dreams and metaphors. The writings of the prophets are profound and filled with great insights, but they are not at the same level as the Five Books of Moses—the Torah.

I am always amazed when unknowing people say that Torah is not a spiritual path, or that Moses was a "lawgiver." Moses had an unparalleled intimate mystical relationship with Hashem. The evidence is in the Torah verses that describe it:

- In Exodus, Hashem bids Moses, Aaron, Aaron's sons, and the seventy elders to come up to Him on Mount Sinai. But then Hashem warns Moses, "Only you and Aaron with you shall ascend, the priests and the nation should not ascend to Y/H/V/H . . ." The others cannot come close; they cannot ascend to that level. The others are vouchsafed a certain level of spiritual elevation, but only Moses and Aaron are accorded a direct personal encounter with Hashem. The Midrash points out that Moses ascended even closer to Y/H/V/H than Aaron.

- In Deuteronomy, Hashem is quoted as saying: "Mouth to mouth I will speak to him and be envisioned, but it won't be a mystery." In other words, when I speak to Moses, it won't be through metaphor, as it was with all the other prophets, patriarchs, and matriarchs.
- The Torah ends with: "There never has been and there never will be a prophet who arises among Israel like Moses, who knew Y/H/V/H face-to-face . . ." This is possibly the most powerful testimonial of the heights of Moses' spiritual achievement.

Many people call me Rabbi. Some call me David. But there's only one person who, when she says, "David," connects to my essence. That's my wife. Nobody says David like my wife says David, because no one can make the connection with me that my wife makes. Rabbi is a colored lense through which people see me, but only my wife sees me through a clear lens.

This is why the Midrash says that Moses' relationship to Hashem was like a wife's to a husband. Moses had a direct, intimate encounter with divine essence, not simply divine presence. He saw Hashem through the clear lens of *tiferet*.

Consider this metaphor from the Kabbalah describing the *tiferet* experience. A king, when he's holding court, wears his royal garments. The world is the royal cloak of Hashem. Perhaps you've seen pictures of wizards wearing a cloak with stars and the moon on it. They were trying to imitate Hashem, because a verse in Psalms describes Hashem as "wearing splendor . . . He has taken light and clothed Himself in the light like a garment, and He has put the skies like a cloak around him."

In other words, when we embrace the world, we're touching the king's cloak. We may feel a presence under the covering, but we are not touching the essence of the king, only his garment.

The king wears his regal garments while presiding in the royal court. But when he retires to the private chambers, he can take off the royal cloak, unbutton his shirt, and slip off his shoes. And then a little more of the private person of the king is revealed. Only with his wife, however, is the king completely uncovered.

Hashem regularly appeared to Moses with no garments, no metaphors, no illusions. It was a direct encounter.

Prophet Isaiah tells us there will be a time when we too will have such an encounter with Hashem: "Your Teacher [Hashem] will no longer engarb himself, and your eyes will literally see Him." It will be so intimate an encounter that only a metaphor of sexual union can describe the closeness.

What makes for the intimacy of such an encounter?

The answer is the naked truth. This is the "color" of *tiferet*—it is translucent.

Getting Real

Tiferet would be best described as the quality of realness, the quality of the genuine, the essential. This is why the Kabbalah refers to *tiferet* as truth. Through the colorless lens of *tiferet,* you see Hashem in truth—it is the naked truth, face-to-face, authentic, genuine.

How do we access this level of truth?

Through the Torah.

The vehicle to get a glimpse of Hashem's face is to soulfully learn Torah. Since Hashem revealed the Torah at Mount Sinai in a direct face-to-face way, it has the power to access for us a glimpse of that original encounter.

The Kabbalah teaches that the Torah embodies the light of Hashem's face. However, if you want to tap that light you have to immerse yourself in the text, get involved with it. You can't just read it or even study it like any other book. To get a glimpse of Hashem's face through the text you have to plug into it.

Generally when we read or study a book, it is in order to acquire the wisdom in it. We are not so concerned with the author as with the wisdom expressed in the book. That is not the case with the Torah. We don't read or study Torah just to access its wisdom, we get involved with it to meet its author—Hashem. Torah is not just a book of wisdom. It is a window to Hashem.

Through contemplation of nature and history we see Hashem from behind, but through involvement in Torah we get a glimpse of the light of Hashem's face. The Torah captures the face-to-face experience that happened at Sinai. If we know how to plug into the text we can relive Sinai today and everyday.

When I was in high school, I did poorly in English literature even though I excelled in other subjects. I just couldn't take English literature seriously. The problem was my attitude. Typically, the teacher would assign a chapter of some great classic for us to read over the weekend. In Monday's class she would ask, "Did you notice the green light flashing across the bay? What was the author expressing in these metaphors?"

I would put up my hand and answer, "The author was probably sitting in his cottage looking out his window as he wrote this chapter and he probably saw a green light flashing across the bay, so he decided to stick it into his story."

Needless to say that is not what the teacher wanted to hear. "David," she'd say sternly, "stop being an annoyance. You know very well that is not the case."

I'd shoot back, "Why not? How do you know why he put that in?"

"He put that in because water represents instability, the color green symbolizes 'go,' and flashing hints at hesitation. The character is feeling this conflict and the scene is reflecting his inner dilemma."

"But how do you know? Did the author tell you that?" I just would not accept the validity of all these subjective interpretations.

But is this not the same problem with the Torah? There are so many commentaries and different interpretations. For centuries sages have poured over the words of the Torah and offered new interpretations. How do we know all their interpretations are right? Especially when they are all so different.

Here lies one of the great differences between Torah and any other book. With other books, unless the author tells me what he meant, I don't know what he meant. It will be subject to my interpretation. But when you immerse your self in Torah, the author, Hashem, personally tells you what He meant.

How so? According to the Kabbalah, you are a soul, the true you is a spark of Hashem. Therefore, when you immerse your true self in Torah, it is as if to say that the author continues to study his own book through the reader, because the reader is actually a spark of the author himself. Therefore Hashem reveals to you new meanings for the Torah every day when you immerse yourself in the text. Every time you open the Torah, you can meet Hashem face-to-face. And then every interpretation that comes to your mind is actually revelatory.

Of course, this doesn't mean you can just say anything you want and distort the text. You must acquire the skills and intentions necessary to properly explore the text with your soul so that you can open the channel for new revelations. To acquire these skills you need a teacher.

The Torah embodies truth. Through its teachings and guidance it puts us in touch with reality, it sets us face-to-face with Hashem. When we embody Torah we embody truth, we become real and connect face-to-face to the One who is real.

Talking It Out

Tiferet is truth but it is also described as beauty. A person who is beautiful is beautiful in whatever garments he or she wears. That's why a sportswear company will pay tens of thousands of dollars to a gorgeous model to wear its blue jeans and T-shirt, and people will clamor to buy those blue jeans and T-shirt, although they won't look as good on them as they do on the model. The model brings beauty to the clothes she is wearing, but customers are deluded into thinking that the clothes are beautiful.

True beauty is the real you coming out, shining through your attributes. *Tiferet,* which reveals the ungarbed Divine essence, brings beauty to all the other *sefirot.* In other words, it is incorrect to think that what is beautiful is true; rather, what is true is beautiful. And when you face the truth you actually face Hashem. To bring the light of Hashem's face into the world we must be truthful, genuine, and honest; then everything is beautiful.

Tiferet is also associated with encountering Hashem as "You." That is, I can talk about a person who is not in the room as "him" or "her," but I can only address that person as "you" when he or she is standing directly in front of me.

When speaking about the other *sefirot,* we can describe them in terms of Hashem as the Master, Conductor, Lover, Judge. You don't have to talk to Hashem to encounter the conductor or to recognize the presence of a supervisor manifesting through nature. But to encounter Hashem through *tiferet,* you have to talk directly to Hashem.

That's the quality of realness that *tiferet* represents. Hashem isn't real until you speak directly to Hashem. You can get a glimpse of kindness or justice just by becoming conscious of the moral imperative within you. And you can get a glimpse of mastery and magnificence by contemplating this wondrous world around you. But Y/H/V/H you have to seek. Someone can show you all the other qualities, but no one can show you *tiferet*. You have to seek it out for yourself. Therefore a verse in Deuteronomy promises: "And you shall seek Y/H/V/H, and you will find." To glimpse *tiferet,* to glimpse Hashem's realness, to experience the light of the divine countenance, you have to seek Hashem out and talk to Hashem directly.

It's something like the way matches were traditionally made in Jewish society. Yonkle's mother would approach Hinda's mother and suggest a match between their children. Yonkle's mother would describe her son as best she could. Then Hinda's mother would do her research. She would ask Yonkle's rabbi, his neighbors, his friends, "What kind of boy is Yonkle?" If, after she found out everything she could about Yonkle and the match seemed appropriate, Hinda's mother would arrange for Yonkle and Hinda to have a face-to-face meeting. Many people have the misconception that such brides and grooms meet for the first time under the marriage canopy. In truth, the law is that the prospective bride and groom have to see each other face-to-face at least one time before they become betrothed. Before they actually meet, Hinda might come to know everything imaginable about Yonkle. She may know his medical history, his personal history, his likes and dislikes, how he relates to his younger sisters, and how he fell from a tree and broke his arm at age seven. Someone may have even pointed Yonkle out on the street for Hinda, so that she knows what he looks like. But there can be no betrothal until she encounters him face-to-face and addresses him as "you." That's *tiferet.*

What does Hinda finally do when she encounters Yonkle sitting on the couch in her parents' drawing room? She talks to him.

It is just the same when we directly encounter Hashem—we talk to Him. That's prayer. And the more you're able to speak to Hashem in prayer, addressing Hashem as "You," the more likely that Hashem will speak to you.

In prayer, we actually do say "You" to Hashem dozens of times each day, every time we pray. Many prayers typically start and conclude with: "Blessed are You, Hashem."

Who am I to say "You" to Hashem? That's an amazing realization. When addressing people of high station—a judge, a president, the queen of England—you are supposed to say "Mr. President," "Your Honor," "Your Majesty." It would be impertinent to say to such a person, "What do you want?" Yet, despite all the references to Hashem as the Master of the Universe, in prayer we actually say, "You" to Hashem.

This is astonishing.

One of the Proverbs states: "As a face is to the water, so is the heart of a person to the heart of another person."

This means that when we approach each other in intimacy—heart-to-heart—we reflect each other.

If you want to encounter Hashem's essence, then you have to be willing to expose your own essence to Hashem. Hashem can only reflect what you're presenting. If you present yourself with genuineness, with authenticity—your beauty in truth—then you reveal your essence and the essence of Hashem will be revealed to you. You have to be real to see the Real.

My tour, as it were, of the *sefirot* stops at the threshold of *tiferet*. You have to go the rest of the way yourself. Even if I were the world's best optometrist, I could not fit you with the clear lens of *tiferet*. You have to seek that direct encounter with Hashem. No one can do it for you. "And you shall seek Y/H/V/H and you will find." To enter the inner private chambers of Hashem, you have to make the journey alone.

If Yonkle and Hinda would decide to get married, the whole town would turn out for their wedding. Throngs of people would crowd around their marriage canopy. But when the wedding ceremony was over, the couple would still not be officially married. The final step is that the bride and the groom be alone together for a period of time in a designated, closed room. So, after the ceremony, the throngs of people accompany the couple, amid much singing and dancing, to the door of this room. But only the bride and groom enter. In fact, two witnesses have to inspect the room first to guarantee to the couple that no one else is hiding there. Aloneness is the crucial element. Yonkle's parents, Hinda's parents, the matchmaker, everyone who was involved in setting up the match, would have to stand outside the door. The real encounter must take place totally alone.

You have to access *tiferet* on your own.

There is really not a lot more I can tell you about *tiferet*. I can only encourage you to go forward. Talk to Hashem, soulfully learn Torah. And listen. And watch a new miraculous world unfold before your eyes.

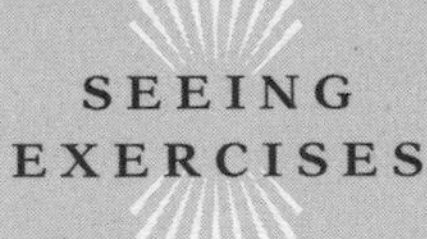

SEEING EXERCISES

1. Can you remember a time when you experienced Hashem's presence?
2. Can you remember a time when you encountered the Divine essence?
3. Who do you know who can really call you by name and encounter your essence? If you know no one, then describe the kind of person you would trust with your name and you would want to encounter face-to-face?
4. Try and immerse yourself in one of the stories in the Torah. What does this story mean to you? What lesson do you see for yourself in that story?
5. Can you think of a time when you were kind but not truthful, or just but not truthful? What's the difference?
6. Can you remember a time when you spoke soulfully to Hashem? What did you achieve by doing that?
7. Can you remember a time when you felt you showed your essence to someone? What conditions do you feel you need in order to feel comfortable in doing that? How do you think you can help others in this regard?

nine

SEEING THE ONE WHO SEES

Now we are going to explore three remaining *sefirot—keter,* which literally means "crown," *hokhma,* "wisdom," and *binah,* "understanding."

Where does will come from? Where does thought come from? Where does intelligence come from? Where does intuition come from? Where does logic come from?

Through these *sefirot* we see that Hashem is the essence and source of will and intellect.

Creative Flash

Hokhma, wisdom, is the innovative, unpredictable force of inspiration and intuition. A sudden flash of knowing. It comes "out of the blue" and usually is experienced as a gift. "It just came to me," we exclaim.

Remember the story of Archimedes? He was trying hard to figure out the scientific principle of the displacement of water. No matter how hard he thought, he couldn't solve the problem. Then he was taking a bath, and suddenly, he got it. He was so excited, he jumped out of his bathtub and started running down the street yelling, "Eureka! Eureka!"

Can you remember a time when you had a eureka experience? Maybe you were walking in a shopping mall and suddenly you got a flash. Something hit you. Something you weren't even thinking about. Perhaps the solution to a problem you had given up working on. Perhaps an insight into something that was puzzling you. *Hokhma* is this creative, intuitive lightning bolt. The lightning flashes, and you get an idea.

It's interesting that we use the term, "get an idea," implying receiving the idea from outside ourselves. Or we speak of "conceiving an idea." What does conceive mean? Who impregnated me with that idea? Where does this idea come from? Am I the source of it?

Once I was at someone's home for dinner. For the first course they served a food that I'd never seen before. "What is this?" I asked innocently. "Cervelles," the hostess replied. It looked really interesting. I tasted it. "Hmm, what's it made from?" I asked. "Brains." I practically choked. Brains? I was eating brains! So I sat there pondering this glob on my plate. Is this really where all the profound thoughts and lofty ideas of the world come from? I thought. If we opened Einstein's head, would we see the source of all his brilliant conceptions in his cervelles?"

I once saw a mind-boggling documentary. It started with a man walking around a glass case. Inside the glass case the viewer could see a gadget that at pulsing intervals was squirting water on something, apparently to keep it from drying out. After several minutes of contemplatively circling this glass case, whose contents the viewer has not been able to make out, the man starts to talk. "This is my brain," he says. "I have removed my brain so we can get a chance to look at it." All of a sudden he says, "Wait a second." And the viewer realizes that the man is looking at and describing his brain, but he's outside of it. It was a very effective device to jolt the viewer into thinking: "Is the self inside this brain? Where does the self come from? How did the self evolve?"

When I think of the tremendous ingenuity human beings are capable of—the original ideas, the flashes of brilliance—I know it didn't all originate in an amorphous mass of cervelles. Every time I get on an airplane, I start to laugh. I just look at this huge apparatus, weighing how many tons, and I say in wonder, "This thing is actually going to get off the ground? This huge, heavy thing is going to fly in the sky? No way!" And I just spontaneously laugh, like a child who laughs at something new and surprising. Of course, when the flight attendant starts her litany of what to do if the plane crashes, I stop laughing. But my wonder at what human beings have been able to invent, to conceptualize, and to actualize is genuine. Such flashes of brilliance come from *hokhma.* It is the Divine manifesting through the *sefira* of *hokhma*—inspiration and intuition.

Conception

When you look through the lense of *hokhma,* you begin to see the true essence and source of wisdom, of inspiration, of brilliance. Without the lens of *hokhma,* you see only the cervelles as the source of all ideas. I was once having a discussion with a fellow who claimed that he did not believe in spiritual realities. He said, "I don't believe in soul. I don't believe in spirituality. None of that stuff. It's a bunch of garbage."

So I asked him. "How would you describe your relationship with your wife? I mean, is that a spiritual encounter?"

"No," he answered. "It's just neural impulses."

"Have you ever shared that with your wife?" I countered.

Could you imagine this couple having a romantic evening. He says to her, "Sweetheart, your neural impulses are activating my neural impulses."

But if he chooses to think that he is the sum total of his neural impulses, then that will define the nature of his world and his relationships. He will live in a world that is populated by beings who are programmed with various neural impulses.

But when I look at the world through the glasses of *hokhma,* I begin to become aware of Hashem as the source and power behind all brilliance, creativity, and genius. And I become humbly thankful that I am a receptacle, that I am a channel for that idea or that song or that poem to come down into the world. Musicians, artists, and writers often experience this sense that *they* are not doing it, that something is coming *through* them. I knew an artist who, when he had finished painting a picture, had difficulty in signing his name. He didn't feel that it was his, but rather that he had been the instrument for a higher force of creativity. Can the paintbrush take credit for its strokes? Poets often say, "I was moved to write this," or "the spirit moved me," acknowledging a force outside themselves for which they were simply the instrument. Where is all this inspiration coming from? From Hashem—the source of inspiration and intuition.

I used to be a great fan of Bob Dylan, and loved the songs he wrote. Once I heard a radio interviewer who asked, "Bob, how do you write such songs?"

Dylan replied, "I just put my pen on a page, and I just know it's going to be all right."

Now go to school and try to learn how to do that. Try to figure out how to activate your neurons to write beautiful music. That kind of inspiration does not surface on demand. You cannot decide to write a great poem or compose a haunting theme, and presto, you churn it out.

Writers moan about writer's block, when they feel totally uninspired. Even a best-selling novelist can sit at her typewriter and feel frustrated because nothing is coming to her. Coming from where? Did she forget how to type the words? Did she forget all the techniques she learned in creative writing classes? Neurons can fire at will, but creativity comes as a divine gift.

I once met a screenwriter who told me that every day before he sits down to write, he says a little prayer: "Please, God, use me."

Now, of course, the creative flash is not enough, because the idea still has to be processed. It has to be articulated, formulated, structured.

In Kabbalah, inspiration/intuition and logic are compared to the male and the female. *Hokhma* is compared to the seed—that microscopic, one-celled drop—that the male implants in the female, *binah.* But there the seed must develop into a myriad of complex details.

In an instant, Thomas Edison got the flash to turn electricity into usable light. But then he had to develop his idea and painstakingly try different kinds of filaments until he produced an actual lightbulb. That mental process of development, elaboration, and analysis comes from *binah.*

Have you ever had an experience where you knew you knew the answer, but you didn't know what it was? Have you ever been in class where the teacher threw out a question, and you shot up your hand, but when the teacher called on you, all you could say was, "Uhm, uh, uh . . ."?

When your hand went up, that was *hokhma.* You had that flash, you had that seed, but you didn't take time to really call it out, formulate it into words, draw out the concept. *Binah* had not come into play.

When I was in rabbinical school, my learning partner and I would sometimes struggle over a difficult piece of Talmud. We would both be staring at the page, and suddenly, in perfect synchronicity, we would yell out, "I got it!" Then I would say to him, "You go ahead and explain it."

"No," he'd say, "you go ahead," looking a bit sheepish.

"OK, one second!" I'd stall.

Then we would both put our heads down again. A few minutes later, we would both be able to articulate it. What happened? Didn't we get it the first time? The first time is the experience of *hokhma.* But it hasn't evolved. Understanding it, giving it structure, and filling it in is *binah.*

The power of *hokhma,* which is intuitive, holistic, and experiential, is manifested in our right brain. The power of *binah,* which is analytical, logical, and rational, is manifested in our left brain. But the source of all is the one and only Hashem, Who chooses to be manifested in the full spectrum of the Divine light shining through us.

The Will

Keter is literally translated as "crown" and also suggests "that which encompasses." However, it conceptually refers to the cosmic power of will and consciousness.

We will first examine *keter* in relationship to will.

Will is a very difficult concept to explain, yet we have all experienced it. No scientist has ever been, or probably ever will be, able to isolate, formulate, and analyze what will is. Where does it come from?

If you were to lift your right hand, a scientist would be able to trace the path of the neurons that commanded your muscles to do the physical action of lifting your hand. But who commanded the neurons? The brain? No, your will did.

Will is bombarding us all the time. For me to be sitting at the computer writing this, I have to have will. For me to speak, I have to have will. For me to want to go to sleep, I have to have will. Everything needs will. Without will, the game is over. Will is really the source and essence of all life forces. If a person loses the will to live, he or she dies. Of course, legends are full of tragic heroes and heroines who die of a broken heart, but contemporary medical research has shown in scores of tests that many diseases are statistically related to depression, loss, emotional trauma, and other factors that nullify a person's will to live.

What motivates an ant to walk up a wall carrying in its jaws a crumb many times its own weight? What is the source of the enormous determination of such a tiny insect? What is the driving force?

It's a mystery. We know so little about it. We know that what we will is our choice. But that we have will at all is not our choice. I have the choice of what I want to do with my will, but is will itself really my own?

Imagine yourself as a pipe. Water is flowing into you. You as a pipe can turn left or right and direct the water to flow in several different directions. But you can't determine whether or not the water will flow into you.

So too will is flowing into us all the time. Which way we channel it, into which activities we invest it, is our choice. But we have no choice whether or not to have choice. Ironically, we are compelled to have choice; even not making a choice is a choice.

When I begin to look at the world through the lens of *keter,* cosmic will, I begin to be very sensitive to its presence. For the first time, I look around and see that everything has will.

Who is the source of the colossal power of will that fills the world? Cosmogonical theories such as the Big Bang account only for physical reality, but what accounts for nonphysical realities such as will? When you really start to ponder the power of will, the mystery of will, you begin to see that Hashem is the source and essence of all will.

Life on Loan

The name of Hashem associated with *keter* is *Ehyeh.* We see this name in the Torah in the dialogue at the burning bush, when Moses has been assigned by Hashem to bring the Jewish people out of Egypt. Moses asks Hashem: "If they ask me, 'Who is this God that's sending you?' what should I say?" Hashem replies, "*Ehyeh asher Ehyeh.* I am that I am. Therefore you shall say to them 'I am' sent you." This is one of the Divine names, the great "I am"—*Ehyeh.*

"I am" means that Hashem is the one and only totally self-determined reality, the source and master of all will. "I am" also means pure consciousness, the source of all awareness.

On its most basic level, consciousness or awareness is the ability to say, "I am." That fundamental awareness of our own existence, before any thought process, logic, or rationality, is also the power of *keter* manifesting in each one of us.

But where does awareness come from? What is its source?

Am I the source of awareness? Did the self beget itself? Did awareness start with me? Will it end with me? Do I own it? Am I the master of it? Did I create it? Did I earn it? Obviously not. Therefore, I cannot say, "I am that I am." The most fundamental components of my identity, which are my will, my consciousness, and my life, do not belong to me. They came as a gift, and they can be taken away from me at any moment. I cannot claim that my life is mine, or that my mind is my own.

The Talmud relates a powerful episode in the life of Rabbi Meir and his wife Bruria, who was a great scholar in her own right and whose opinions are quoted in the Talmud. One Shabbat, the couple's two beloved young sons suddenly took sick and died. Rabbi Meir was not at home at the time. Bruria lay her sons' bodies lovingly in an upper room and covered them, determined that the tragic loss should not mar her husband's Sabbath peace. When Rabbi Meir returned home and inquired as to where the boys were, Bruria made an excuse for their absence. Once the Sabbath was over at sundown, Bruria had the terrible task of breaking the tragic news to her husband. And she did it by posing a question to him: "Years ago, someone left me precious jewels to take care of. Now he has come to collect his jewels. How should I feel? Must I give them back?" Thinking that she was just asking for a legal opinion, Rabbi Meir answered immediately, "Of course. You must return them to their owner without hesitation and you should feel satisfied that you have faithfully guarded these jewels and are able to return them to their true owner." Bruria then led him to the upper room and said, "Hashem left two beautiful jewels in our care. Today He came and took them back."

It is difficult to really feel that our children's lives do not belong to us. In truth, even our own lives are really "on loan." It's a great mistake when people say, "It's my life, so I can do with it what I please." Hashem is the only one who can state, "I am that I am."

To Own or Owe

When you go to the optometrist, and you come out with a new prescription for your glasses or contact lenses, you are suddenly able to see things you never saw before. Similarly, through the lens of *keter,* you will start to see will and consciousness, and you will realize that nothing you have is really yours. That's a very high level. It gives people a tremendous amount of peace.

On the one hand, it's important to know when the world is falling apart and to do what you can to help. On the other hand, it's just as important to remember that it's not your world. You can certainly play a role in making the world better, in bringing peace and healing into it. But it's not your world.

I've met people who have a Hercules complex: They think they are carrying the world on their shoulders. As long as there is one toxic waste site to clean up or one whale to save, they can't relax. But who is really the owner of this world?

Imagine a very dedicated, responsible employee of a large shoe company. The owner of the shoe company goes away on a three-week vacation and leaves this employee in charge. Of course, the employee has to shoulder the responsibility for everything: production, supplies, meeting orders on schedule, advertising, sales, and so forth. He has to handle every crisis, make weighty decisions, and sweat out every problem, because during those three weeks it's his company. There is no other boss. Then the owner comes back. Does the employee put his feet up on the desk and stop working? No, he resumes his duties and performs them carefully and energetically, but he is no longer carrying the responsibility for the whole company. On evenings and weekends, he can let go and relax with his family.

That's what happens when you put on the lens of *keter* and see that the company has an owner: Hashem. You may have thought you were in charge of everything, but as soon as you see the real owner, you relax a little. You don't goof off and become a beach bum; you continue to do your job with dedication and perhaps even more zeal, but relinquishing control to the real owner is very liberating; it brings you peace.

When people fall into the misunderstanding that "it is my life," something often happens that forces them to realize that they are not in control. Unfortunately, the catalysts are not usually pleasant. Illness, the death of a loved one, losing a job, disappointment in a relationship, all lead one to realize that one is not in control. It is a painfully acquired awareness. Such events confer on us the lens of *keter,* the perception of reality as it is.

Of course this realization doesn't have to be achieved through pain. It can be done through the weekly celebration of the Sabbath. We can take one day out of the week and give the world back to Hashem. In this way we demonstrate that we are aware that we are not creators of this world, we are not the boss, we just work here. And if the boss wants to close up shop one day a week then there is no reason for me to go to work.

The Endless Circuit

When I begin to look at the world through the lens of *keter,* I become sensitive to ultimate will, and consciousness. I realize that my own will and consciousness is only a drop in the ocean of universal will and consciousness. I realize that life has been entrusted to me. It is a trust fund. I don't own it, but I administer it faithfully and responsibly.

True will is participation in Divine Will. True awareness is participation in Divine Mind. True life is actually participation in Divine Life. We don't own them, we only participate.

If I am not the owner of will and consciousness, only a participant, then who am I?

The truth is that the self is the most elusive, most difficult to cognize. Why is this so? Because the self is that which is seeing. The eyes cannot see themselves.

When people complain that they can't see Hashem, often they think this is because Hashem is so far away, up in the distant heavens. But the real reason is because Hashem is too close to us.

It says in the Talmud, "Just as the soul sees, and yet is unseen, so too is Hashem sees, and yet is unseen." The soul is what is seeing and therefore it cannot be seen. So too is Hashem. In other words, to see Hashem you would have to see the source of all seeing. Through *yesod, hod, netzah, gevurah, hesed,* and *tiferet* we can see right before our eyes manifestations of Hashem in life, nature, history, love, kindness, justice, and truth. But above and beyond that, we cannot see Hashem before our eyes, but rather we experience Hashem *behind* our eyes.

Through *keter, hokhma,* and *binah* we experience Hashem as the source of all seeing and of all knowing. This intimate level of knowing Hashem is participation in Hashem's self-knowledge. You are plugging into a circuit of divine self-knowledge.

The Torah teaches that Hashem is "the knower, the knowing, and the known." In other words, when you think about yourself, you are both the subject (the knower) and the object (the known), and of course the whole process of knowing is within you. Therefore the knower, the knowing, and the known are one.

However, the truth is that only Hashem is the knower, the knowing, and the known, because only Hashem is the source of all consciousness. To know Hashem you must participate in the circuit of Hashem's own self-knowledge. A circuit that starts with Hashem and returns to Hashem.

Essentially, thinking about Hashem is like trying to plug into Hashem thinking about Himself. It is trying to participate in an inner Divine process. When you achieve that, you experience Hashem not as the object of your thoughts, but as the subject of all thoughts.

The *keter* experience is associated with the ultimate no-thing because there is no word that can describe the source of all knowledge. It's actually a very lofty no-thing, meaning that this reality is so great, so beyond everything knowable that it doesn't fit into any category. No words can describe it; it cannot be compared to anything.

Hashem is the source of all knowledge and the source of all consciousness and the source of all will and the source of all words and the source of all thoughts. Clearly, the source of all thoughts and words cannot be described by thoughts and words, just as the eye cannot see itself. Therefore, when I'm asked to think of Hashem, I should draw a blank, a total blank. Because I realize that there is absolutely no word and no concept to capture the source of all consciousness. Therefore I reach the ecstatic experience of nothingness. I experience myself as existing within Hashem's endless field of consciousness. At that moment, I experience myself as participating in Hashem's endless process of self-knowledge.

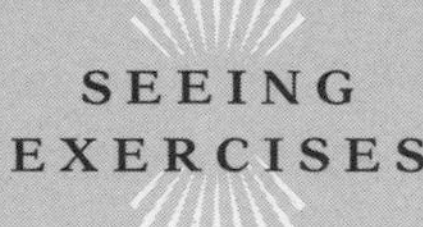

SEEING EXERCISES

1. Can you recall an inspirational idea, or an intuitive or creative flash that came to you recently?
2. Can you remember one such idea that actually changed your life?
3. Today, perhaps on your way to work, look for brilliance, creativity, or inspiration around you. Take a little time to reflect on and appreciate how someone's ingenuity has improved your life—for example, contemplate the fluorescent light on the subway train, or the sliding doors, or your wristwatch.
4. As you try to think of these manifestations of brilliance and ingenuity, pay attention to the process by which ideas pop into your head.
5. Try and recall a time when you arrived at the solution to a problem. Can you describe exactly how it happened or did it just happen?
6. Did you ever experience getting an idea at the very same moment as your friend sitting next to you did? Did you ever find someone "taking the words right out of your mouth" and saying exactly what you were about to say?
7. Can you remember an idea that came to you after much effort and logical analysis?
8. Take a little time today to appreciate the miracle of your will. Focus on different muscles in your body and move

them. Try your left toe. Now try both your left and right toe simultaneously. Now raise your right eyebrow while pressing your tongue into your left cheek. Where did you acquire the power to do this? Who taught you how to do it?

9. Close your eyes and imagine a time (a) when you didn't have the motivation or didn't like doing something, and (b) when you were charged with willpower and drive. What made the difference?
10. Close your eyes and watch the stream of ideas as they appear before you. Don't hang on to any one of them; just let them flow by. Notice how many ideas are constantly popping into your mind. Now take a moment to appreciate the field of awareness in which all this is happening. Be aware of awareness itself.
11. Can you remember an event in your life when you realized "it is not my life" and when you just had to let go?
12. Is there a situation in your life right now that you are trying to control and that is causing you much stress? Can you let go and trust Hashem that it will be all right?

epilogue

For years I pondered, contemplated, and grappled with how to know God, but none of that got me closer to my goal. I ended up with a philosophy full of lifeless ideas and dead concepts. I then realized that to know God I would have to find Him, meet Him. But where was I to look?

It took me a little more time and a lot more frustration to realize that to find God I had to stop looking. I needed to simply open my eyes and see Him right here and now. If I could not see God "here" and "now," I would not see Him "there" or "later" either.

I challenged myself and asked: If you can't see God in the wonders of nature, in the flowers, the trees, the setting of the sun, then where will you see Him? God is the source and soul of nature.

If you can't see God in acts of love, kindness, and justice, where will you see Him? God is the source and soul of morality and ethics.

If you can't see God in the very mystery of seeing at all, where will you see Him? God is the source and soul of all awareness.

What made this so difficult was that it was so simple. We are accustomed to very complicated ideas. We have forgotten the simple skill of seeing with our soul—spiritual seeing.

I was fortunate to find the teachings of the Torah and Kabbalah to show me the way.

The first step to opening the eyes of your soul is to realize that there is no such thing as God. God is a lifeless caricature, described as an invisible being floating in space. This false image is obstructing the eyes of our soul. We have to get rid of God in order to see Hashem—the Ultimate Reality Who embraces everything and fills everything.

To see Hashem we must learn to see allness with the eyes of wonder. Hashem is the whole of reality, greater than the sum of the parts. The more expansive and encompassing our vision, the more we are able to see Hashem.

Hashem is absolutely unique and incomparable to anything we know. To see Hashem we must see with the eyes of wonder—without expectations—to see what we have never seen before. Seeing with the eyes of wonder is seeing for the first time every time. The truth of Hashem is believable as soon as life becomes unbelievable. Learn to live in amazement.

However, true spiritual seeing cannot be done alone. We are not independent, isolated islands of mind. We are all interrelated and interdependent. Therefore, we are only able to see Hashem when we are part of a collective communal consciousness. Community is absolutely necessary for opening the eyes of the soul.

The Kabbalah teaches that there are ten qualities to Hashem. These qualities are referred to as the ten *sefirot*. These qualities cannot be understood in a philosophical way. They must be experienced. They are no-things. They are like colors and flavors. When you see it or taste it, you'll know.

The more we acknowledge these Divine qualities in the way we act, speak, and think, the more we channel them into our world. If we do not see Hashem, then Hashem will not be in our world or in our lives.

The first *sefira* is called *malhus*—kingdom. This is the collective community consciousness that is the necessary lens to see the other Divine qualities.

Yesod is life, goodness, and blessing. Life is the synergy of all the other Divine qualities. Through *yesod* we see Hashem in life.

Our daily life mission is to connect *malhus* with *yesod*. We achieve personal fulfillment when we are contributive members of a collective communal awareness of Hashem. We become live wires bringing Hashem's light into the world when we recognize and embody the full spectrum of Divine qualities that make up the true goodness and blessing of life.

Netzah is mastery, and *hod* is magnificence. Through *netzah* and *hod* we see Hashem in the marvelous synchronicity of nature and daily events—in Divine Providence.

Gevurah is justice, and *hesed* is kindness. Through the perfect balance of *gevurah* and *hesed* we see Hashem in love.

Tiferet is truth and beauty. Through *tiferet* we get a glimpse of Divine essence, we get a taste of the face-to-face intimacy with Hashem. Through *tiferet* we meet Hashem: we speak to Him through prayer, and He speaks to us through Torah study.

Binah is logical analytical thinking, and *hokhma* is the creative flash of inspiration and intuition. Through *binah* and *hokhma* we encounter Hashem in the very process of all intellect and understanding. We discover that we are participants in a Divine process that does not start or end with us. We realize that Hashem is not only the ultimate object of knowledge, as in the other *sefirot,* but also the ultimate subject of all knowledge. Hashem is, therefore, the source, context, ground, and goal of all knowing. He is the knower, the knowing, and the known. Our ultimate joy and fulfillment is to be like cables to connect this circuit, vehicles for this mysterious process of Hashem's self-knowledge.

Keter is the ultimate source and ground of all will and consciousness. Through *keter* we encounter Hashem in the very existence of will and awareness. We become aware of awareness and marvel at the mystery of free will. We now know that Hashem is the root of "I am-ness," of self-determination and awareness. We discover that our will and mind is really not ours. We realize that all that we seem to own is really on loan. And we trust.

The Kabbalah teaches us that Hashem is right here, right now, waiting to be seen, wanting to be known. All we have to do is open our eyes to see, open our hearts to feel, and open our minds to know.

Together we can turn every ordinary place, event, and meeting into an extraordinary opportunity to see Hashem. If not now, when?

Dear Reader,

Thank you for joining me on this spiritual sight-seeing adventure. Although you have reached the end of this book, this soulful adventure never ends.

Please write me. It will be an honor and privilege to receive your comments and questions.

All the best,

David Aaron

Isralight Institute
25 Misgav Ladach
Old City, Jerusalem
97500 Israel
e-mail: david.aaron@isralight.org
See Rabbi David Aaron live at http://www.isralight.org.

PHOTO BY DAVID HAAS

David Aaron is the founder and dean of the Isralight Institute, an international organization with centers in Israel and the United States. He travels throughout the world lecturing and leading retreats. Spiritual mentor to many, including several celebrities, he is also the author of *Endless Light*. He lives in the Old City of Jerusalem with his wife and their six children.